YOUR LIFE

John Foster

2

The
complete course
for **PSHE**
and
Citizenship

Published by HarperCollins*Publishers* Ltd
77–85 Fulham Palace Road
London W6 8JB

www.**Collins**Education.com
On-line support for schools and colleges

First published 2000

Reprinted 2001

ISBN 0 00 327356 3

John Foster asserts the moral right to be identified as the author of this work.

British Library Cataloguing in Publication Data
A catalogue record for this book is available from the British Library.

Commissioned by Thomas Allain-Chapman
Project management by Gaynor Spry
Edited by Kim Richardson
Picture research by Suzanne Williams
Editorial assistant Charlie Evans
Design and layout by Ken Vail Graphic Design, Cambridge
Illustrations by Bethan Matthews
Cover design by Ken Vail Graphic Design, Cambridge
Cover photographs: Telegraph Colour Library
Production by Katie Morris
Printed and bound by Printing Express Ltd., Hong Kong

Acknowledgements

The publishers gratefully acknowledge the following for permission to reproduce copyright material. Every effort has been made to trace copyright holders, but in some cases has proved impossible. The publishers would be happy to hear from any copyright holder that has not been acknowledged.

'Coping with shyness' (p8) is adapted from 'Pain of shyness' in T2, *The Daily Telegraph*, 23 October 1999, © Telegraph Group Limited, 1999, used with permission; 'Coping with classroom mistakes' (p9) is adapted from *Wise Guides: Self Esteem* by Anita Naik, published by Hodder & Stoughton, reprinted with permission of Hodder & Stoughton Publishers; 'Drugs – facts and fictions' (p10) is adapted from pp32-35 of *Wise Guides: Drugs* by Anita Naik, published by Hodder & Stoughton, reprinted with permission of Hodder & Stoughton Publishers; 'Is cannabis safe?' (p10) and 'Drugs and the law' (p12) are taken from *The Score – Facts about Drugs* © Health Education Authority, used with permission; 'How to turn down drugs and stay friends' (p13) is from pp36-38 of *Wise Guides: Drugs* by Anita Naik, published by Hodder & Stoughton, reprinted with permission of Hodder & Stoughton Publishers; table 'The ethnic composition of Britain' (p14) is from *Roots of the Future* published by Commission for Racial Equality, reprinted with permission; 'Stereotype' (p15) by John Agard is from *Mangoes and Bullets* published by Pluto Press (1985), reprinted by kind permission of John Agard c/o Caroline Sheldon Literary Agency; 'Films and TV programmes' (p16), 'The press' (p17) and 'Only joking?' (p17) are from *Life Files: Racism* by Jagdish Gundara and Roger Hewitt, published by Evans Brothers Limited, copyright © Evans Brothers Limited 1999, used with permission; 'TV failing to reflect multicultural society' (p16) is from a report by Janine Gibson in *The Guardian*, 8 December 1999, © The Guardian, reprinted with permission; 'A distorted picture' (p17) is from *Speaking Out – Black Girls in Britain* by Audrey Osler, published in the Virago Upstarts series, reprinted with permission of the author; 'Fruit machine facts' (p19) is from 'Shout report – gambling' in *Shout* issue 127, published by D. C. Thomson & Co. Ltd, copyright © D. C. Thomson & Co. Ltd, reprinted with permission; 'Problem gambling' (p21) is adapted from *A Certain Bet* published by GamCare, reprinted with permission; 'Responsible gambling' (p21) is from *Gambling! A Guide for Young People* published by GamCare, reprinted with permission; 'Short wants overseas aid reform bill' (p24) from *Daily Telegraph*, 6 January 2000, 'Pay-out for man denied bar job over his ponytail' (p24) from *Daily Express*, 14 January 2000, and 'Owners of airguns face curbs' (p25) from *Daily Telegraph*, 12 January 2000, © Telegraph Group Limited, used with permission; 'Blair to support police on stop laws' (p24) from *Sunday Times*, 16 January 2000, and 'Dolly man to clone herd of 1,500 cows' (p25) from *Sunday Times*, 9 January 2000, © Times Newspapers Limited, 2000, used with permission; '25 species that could vanish' (p25) from *The Express*, 12 January 2000, 'Straw backs down over boxer for the money-makers' (p24) from *The Express*, 14 January 2000, 'Moves to relax the laws on cannabis' (p24) from *The Express*, 14 January 2000, and 'Get on your bikes and cut the traffic jams, pupils are urged' (p25) from *The Express*, 14 January 2000, are used with permission; 'GM ban is extended by Tesco' (p25) is from *The Guardian*, 7 January 2000, © The Guardian 2000, used with permission; 'Dealing with divorce' (p26) is from *Girls Know Best* compiled by Michelle Roehm, published by Beyond Words Publishing Inc. © copyright 1997 by Beyond Words Publishing Inc., Hillsboro, Oregon, USA, used with permission; 'We had to move to a small flat' and 'I get the best of both worlds' (p28) are from *Dealing with Family Break-Up* by Kate Haycock, published by Wayland Publishers, reprinted with permission of Hodder & Stoughton Publishers; 'I want to be with my mates' (p28) and quotes by Janet, Jason and Rachel (p29) are from *Caught in the Middle* by Alys Swan-Jackson, published by Piccadilly Press, reprinted with permission of Piccadilly Press; 'How to cope with step-parents' (p29) is from 'Coping with step-families' in *Shout* issue 118, published by D. C. Thomson & Co. Ltd, copyright © D. C. Thomson & Co. Ltd, reprinted with permission; 'What is child abuse' (p32) and 'What happens next?' (p33) are from *Speaking out about Abuse – What Every Young Person Should Know* produced by NSPCC, London, reprinted with permission; cartoon (p32) by Corinne Pearlman is from *Speaking out about Abuse – What Every Young Person Should Know* produced by NSPCC, London, reproduced by permission of Corinne Pearlman; 'I feel so guilty and ashamed' (p33) is from *Sussed and Streetwise* by Jane Goldman, published by Piccadilly Press, reprinted with permission of Piccadilly Press; 'Staying safe in the street' (p34) is from *Respect – Your Life Your Choice* published by National Children's Safety Books, used with permission of The Access Partnership, Stockport; 'Safety in public places', 'If someone talks to you persistently' and 'The golden rule of self-defence' (p35) are from *Stand up for Yourself* by Helen Benedict, published by Hodder & Stoughton, reprinted with permission of Hodder & Stoughton Publishers, and Helen Benedict; 'Police duties and police powers' (p38), 'Helping the police' (p39) and 'Raves' (p40) are from *Young Citizen's Passport – Your Guide to the Law* published by Hodder & Stoughton Limited, reprinted with permission of Hodder & Stoughton Limited; 'Reprimands, warnings and prosecutions' (p39) is from a leaflet *Youth Justice* produced by the Metropolitan Police Youth Justice Task Force 1999, reprinted with permissio of the Metropolitan Police Service; 'Doing a good job?' (p41) is from *Teen Law* published by Quest, A Your Enterprise Company, Queen Elizabeth Boys School, used with permission; 'The secret of making friends' (p42) is from *Friends and Enemies* by Anita Naik, published by Hodder & Stoughton, reprinted with permission of Hodder & Stoughton Publishers; 'The rules of friendship' (p43) is from *Play Stay Keep Safe* published by National Children's Safety Books, used with permission of The Access Partnership, Stockport 'Growing apart' (p43) is from *Shout Summer Special*, 1999, published by D. C. Thomson & Co. Ltd, copyrigh © D. C. Thomson & Co. Ltd, reprinted with permission; 'How much are you influenced by your friends?' (p44) is adapted from *Exploring Healthy Sexuality* by Cathy Jewitt, Family Planning Association, used with permission; 'Gangs – know the facts' (p45) is from *Shout* issue 105 published by D. C. Thomson & Co. Ltd, copyright © D. C. Thomson & Co. Ltd, reprinted with permission; 'Is advertising good or bad?' (p46) and 'The commercial break' (p48) are from *Third Stages* by Jim Sweetman, published by Collins Educational, reprinted with permission of HarperCollins Publishers and Jim Sweetman; 'Advertising and children' (p47) is from Appendix 3 of the Radio Authority's Advertising and Sponsorship Code, March 1997, reprinted wit the kind permission of the Radio Authority; 'Celebrity endorsement' (p49) is from a newspaper article by Bryony Gordon in T2, *The Daily Telegraph*, 28 August 1999, © Telegraph Group Limited, used with permission; 'What's all the fuss about?' (p54) is adapted from *Drugs – Reference Point Series* by Anita Ganeri published by Scholastic Limited, reprinted with permission; 'Getting drunk' (p55) is from *A DIY Guide to Sensible Drinking for Young People* published by the Alcohol Advisory Centre, Bristol (ACAD), used with permission; 'Kerry's story' (p56) is from *Shout* issue 116 published by D. C. Thomson & Co. Ltd, copyright D. C. Thomson & Co. Ltd, reprinted with permission; 'Valerie's story' (p57) is from an article 'Stolen childhood' by Anita Chaudhuri in *19*, 19 October 1991; 'Living with someone who drinks – how to cope' (p57) and cartoon 'Drinking is attractive' (p55) are from *Wise Guides: Drugs* by Anita Naik, published by Hodder & Stoughton, reprinted with permission of Hodder & Stoughton Publishers; 'School calendar shake up' (p58) is adapted from 'A fifth term just for fun in school calendar shake-up' by Tony Halpin in *The Daily Mail*, 12 January 2000, used with permission; 'Dentists warn of piercing perils' (p65), adapted from an article 'Dentists warn of illnesses linked to tongue-piercing' in *Daily Telegraph*, 21 July 1999, 'Sickening sight!' (p65), from the letters page of T2, *The Daily Telegraph*, 12 June 1999, and 'Should body piercing be banned?' (p65), adapted from an article in T2, *The Daily Telegraph*, 5 June 1999, © Telegraph Group Limited, used with permission; Zoe Rockliffe's quote (p65) is from 'A piercing cry of anger' in *The Guardian* 25 February 1998, © The Guardian, used with permission; 'I'm worried about protection' (p69) is from 'Yo top 50 problems solved' by Tricia Kreitman © 1997 *MIZZ*; 'The rhythm method' and 'Withdrawal' (p69) an 'Sex myths' (p71) are from *Wise Guides: Sex* by Anita Naik, published by Hodder & Stoughton, reprinted wit permission of Hodder & Stoughton Limited; 'Sexual rights and responsibilities' (p70) is adapted from *Stand up for Yourself* by Helen Benedict, published by Hodder & Stoughton, reprinted by permission of Hodder & Stoughton Publishers and Helen Benedict; 'What is acceptable in a sexual relationship?' (p71) is adapted from *Exploring Healthy Sexuality* by Carey Jewitt, published by Family Planning Association, used with permission; 'How it began' (p72) is from 'Gaining strength through unity' by Larry Elliott, from *Guardian Education*, 26 February 1995, © The Guardian, used with permission; 'The single market' (p73) and 'What being done by the EU to protect the environment?' (p75) are from *What Exactly is Europe?* by Muriel Lamb, published by The European Commission, © European Commission 1997, used with permission; 'European institutions' (p76) is from *Democracy in Action* by Simon Foster, published by HarperCollins Publishers, reprinted with permission by HarperCollins Publishers and Simon Foster; 'Should Britain join the euro' (p7 by Philip Johnston, is from T2, *Daily Telegraph*, 26 June 1999, © Telegraph Group Limited, used with permission; the environmental survey chart (p80) is from *Personal and Social Education and Cross Curricular Themes Year 10*, copyright text © Burnage High School and Manchester City Educational Committee 1994, published by Evans Brothers Limited, 2A Portman Mansions, Chiltern Street, London W1M 1LE, used with permission; 'Changing the way we live' (p81) is from *Local Agenda 21 Handbook* 1999 published by Oxford City Council, reprinted with permission; 'I value my valley' and 'Giving young people a voice' (p82) are fro *Groundwork Today* issue 26, reprinted with permission of Groundwork, Birmingham; 'Change on the estate' (p83) is from *Old Problems, Young Solutions* produced by Groundwork, reprinted with permission of Groundwork, Birmingham; 'Ageism' (p84) is adapted from information supplied by Help the Aged; '82 year old forced to give up job' (p84) is adapted from 'Yoga teacher aged 82 loses her position' by Sean O'Neill, i *Daily Telegraph*, 8 March 2000, © Telegraph Group Limited, used with permission; 'Survey finds two worlds of old age' and the graph 'Problems in retirement' (p85) are from an article by Sarah Hall 'Half over 80s exist on £80 a week or less' in *The Guardian*, 5 October 1999, © The Guardian, used with permission; 'An ageing population' (pp86-7) is from *Future Forecasts – Statistics Book and Thinking Ahead – Assembly Book* in the Debate of the Age Series coordinated by Age Concern, used with permission; 'The foods you eat' (pp8 9) from 'Spoilt for choice' (p90) by John Crace, in *Guardian Education*, 1 February 2000, and 'Overpopulation' (p91) from 'When famine is a constant threat' in *Guardian Education*, 11 December 1999, © The Guardian, used with permission; 'The causes of food shortages and famine' (p90) and 'Unequal shares' (p91) are from *Fighting Famine, Beating Hunger* produced by Christian Aid, reprinted with permission 'The water crisis (p92), 'Life in the cities', 'Women and water' and 'Water wars' (p93) are from 'Water, water everywhere but not a drop to drink' by Paul Brown in *Guardian Education*, 18 March 1997, © The Guardian used with permission; 'How much do you know about water?' (p92) is from *Youth Topics* issue 27 – *Water Works* published by CAFOD, London, reprinted with permission.

Photographs

The publishers would like to thank the following for permission to reproduce photographs (the page number is followed, where necessary, by t-top, b-bottom, l-left, r-right, c-centre).

Action-Plus: 7/Richard Francis, 15/Chris Brown, 23t/Glyn Kirk; Art Directors and Trip: 17tr & 75b/Helene Rogers; Bubbles Photo Library: 10/Nikki Gibbs, 34t/Angela Hampton, 35/Ian West, 52t/Pauline Cutler, 58/Jennie Woodcock, 62/John Powell; Dragon News and Picture Agency: 84tl; GettyOne Stone: 6/Hunter Freeman, 8/Howard Grey, 9/Zigy Kaluzny 13/Laurence Monneret, 21b/Steve Taylor, 22/Lori Adamski Peek, 25/Manoj Shah, 26 & 27/Bruce Ayres, 29/Stewart Cohen, 33/Clarissa Leahy, 42/David Stewart, 43/Marc Dolphin, 44/Laurence Monneret, 45/Philip Condit II, 47/John Millar, 48/Deborah Davis, 50t/Andy Sacks, 52b/Mark Douet, 56/Ian O'Leary, 57/Penny Tweedie, 59l/Ian Shaw, 59r/Andy Sacks, 64/Scott Robinson, 65/Andy Sacks, 67t & 68/Peter Cade, 67b/Zigy Kaluzny, 69/Peter Correz, 70/Simon Norfolk, 71/Nacy Honey, 79/Peter Weber, 81l/ESA/K.Hogan, 84tr/David Young Wolff, 84b/Stephen Rose, 87tr/Stewart Cohen, 87cl/Richard Shock, 87br/Carsten Witte, 88/Roy Botterell, 89/Gary John Norman, 94/Arthur Tilley; Courtesy of Groundwork: 82tl,bl & r/Jenny Barnes, 83r, 83l/Martin I. Ellis Associates; The Kobal Collection: 16t; Photofusion: 12/David Montford, 20l/Mark Campbell, 20r/Paul Baldesare, 28/Ute Klaphake, 34b/Paul Baldesare, 36/Don Gray, 39/David Tothill, 40t/Bob Watkins, 41/G. Montgomery, 60/Gina Glover, 61/Mark Campbell, 77/David Montford, 80/Gina Glover, 86/Sam Tanner, 95/Gina Glover; Press Association/European Press Agency: 11, 18, 24, 73, 76, 78, 90t, 92, 93cr; Press Association 14b/Owen Humphreys, 14c/Michael Stephens, 19/Tim Ockenden, 40b/Deutsche Press-Argentur, 46/Matthew Fearn, 49/Neil Munns, 55/David Giles, 81r/Stefan Rousseau; Rex Features: 14t/Today, 16b, 30, 74/Andy Drysdale, 75t; Still Pictures: 17bl/Hartmut Schwarzbach, 90b/Carlos Guarita/Reportage, 93bl/Nigel Dickinson; Frank Spooner Pictures: 21t/Rotolo/Liaison, 23b/Bernstein; John Walmsley: 38, 50b, 66.

Contents

Your Life

Personal, Social and Health Education				Citizenship
Understanding Yourself	**Keeping Healthy**	**Developing Relationships**	**Developing as a Citizen**	
Your Life 1 ● You and your feelings – anxieties and worries ● You and your time – managing your time ● You and your money – pocket money, budgeting and saving ● You and your achievements – reviewing your progress	● You and your body – growing and changing ● You and your body – smoking ● You and your body – eating and exercise ● You and your body – drugs and drugtaking	● You and your family – getting on with others ● You and other people – bullying ● You and your responsibilities – beliefs, customs and festivals ● You and other people – people with disabilities	● You and the law – children's rights ● You and the community – being a good neighbour ● You as a citizen – Britain's government ● You and the media – the power of television	● You and your opinions – how to express your ideas ● You and your values – right and wrong ● You and global issues – resources, waste and recycling ● You and the community – taking action: raising money for a charity
Your Life 2 ● You and your feelings – self-esteem ● You and your time – making the most of your leisure ● You and your money – gambling ● You and your achievements – reviewing your progress	● You and your body – drinking and alcohol ● You and your body – contraception and safer sex ● You and your safety – at home and in the street ● You and your body – drugs and drugtaking	● You and your family – divided families ● You and other people – friends and friendships ● You and your responsibilities – other cultures and lifestyles ● You and other people – older people	● You and the law – the police ● You and the community – the school as a community ● You as a citizen – of the European Union ● You and the media – the power of advertising	● You and your opinions – speaking your mind ● You and your values – where do you stand? ● You and global issues – food and water ● You and the community – taking action on the local environment
Your Life 3 ● You and your feelings – dealing with loss ● You and your decisions – how to make decisions ● You and your money – banking and ways of saving ● You and your achievements – reviewing your progress	● You and your body – adolescence ● You and your body – safer sex and STIs/AIDS ● You and your body – eating disorders ● You and your body – drugs and drugtaking	● You and your family – becoming an adult ● You and other people – being assertive ● You and your responsibilities – tolerance, prejudice and discrimination ● You and other people – people with mental illnesses	● You and the law – crimes and punishments ● You and the community – local government and local organisations ● You as a citizen – of the world ● You and the media – the power of the press	● You and your opinions – which political party do you support? ● You and your values – human rights issues ● You and global issues – poverty ● You and the community – taking action: pressure groups and campaigning

Introduction

To the student

Your Life 2 is the second of three books which together form a comprehensive course in Personal, Social and Health Education and Citizenship at Key Stage 3 (P7, S1, S2). There are twelve PSHE units and eight Citizenship units. These are divided into four broad groups.

Understanding yourself

The four self-awareness units in *Your Life 2* concentrate on developing your self-knowledge and your ability to manage your emotions, and on how to manage your time and money. 'You and your feelings' focuses on the importance of having good self-esteem and on ways of building up confidence. 'You and your money' explores gambling and the problems that can arise from teenage gambling. 'You and your time' looks at how you spend your leisure time and suggests things you can do to make positive use of your free time. The final unit, 'You and your achievements', provides you with an opportunity to assess your progress during Year 8.

Keeping healthy

These four units are designed to complement the work on health education that you are doing elsewhere in the curriculum. The unit on drugs and drugtaking examines myths about drugs, presents information on ecstasy and drugs law and offers advice on how to say 'No' to drugs. 'You and your safety' explains how to give emergency first aid, what constitutes abuse and the importance of speaking out, how to stay safe in public places and how to cycle safely. The drinking and alcohol unit explains the effects of alcohol, explores attitudes towards drinking and looks at the effects of alcoholism. The unit on contraception and safer sex explains what is involved in having a sexual relationship, what the risks are and how to reduce the risks, what rights and responsibilities people have.

Developing relationships

This strand of the course aims to develop your ability to handle close relationships and to show respect and responsibility in your dealings with other people in the community. 'You and your family' focuses on divided families, examining what children feel when parents separate and how to cope with living in a stepfamily. 'You and your responsibilities' aims to make you aware of the ethnic diversity of modern Britain and of the effects of ethnic stereotyping in the media. There are two units entitled 'You and other people': one is concerned with friends, exploring the nature of friendship and the problems that can arise with friends. The other focuses on older people, examining ageism, exploring what life is like for older people now and what it might be like in the future.

Developing as a citizen

There are eight units in this strand of the course. In the 'You and your values' unit you are asked to consider what influences your behaviour, what makes you view someone as a hero and which of a range of contemporary issues you regard as the most important. 'You and your opinions' offers guidance on how to distinguish between facts and opinions, how to develop your opinions and how to prepare a speech for a debate. 'You and the law' focuses on the police, their duties and powers and people's attitudes towards them. The 'You as a citizen' unit examines what being in the European Union means and explores proposals for the future development of the EU. 'You and the media' investigates the power and influence of advertising. 'You and global issues' examines issues of food production and distribution and of the availability of clean water supplies. There are two units entitled 'You and the community': one focuses on the school as a community, suggesting things you can do to participate fully in the life of the school. The other focuses on the local environment and community action projects to change and improve it.

The various activities within each unit provide opportunities for you to learn how to grow as individuals, for example, by developing self-awareness and taking responsibility for managing your time. The group discussion activities involve you in learning how to co-operate and negotiate. You are presented with situations in which you have to work with others, to analyse information, to consider moral and social dilemmas and to make choices and decisions. By working together on school and community projects you have the chance to participate fully in the life of your school and community and to develop skills that you will require as active citizens.

Self-esteem and confidence

Self-esteem

What is self-esteem?

Self-esteem means having a good opinion of yourself. It is based on understanding what your strengths are and valuing yourself as a person.

Why is self-esteem important?

Self-esteem is important because it enables you to have the confidence to be yourself. If you have self-esteem, you will say what you think and do what you think is right, rather than say or do things in order to try to impress other people.

Having self-esteem will make you feel happier. You won't let people make you feel badly about yourself if they criticise you unfairly. Because you believe in yourself, you'll respect yourself and other people will respect you too. You won't fall into the trap of blaming yourself for everything that goes wrong in your life.

Self-esteem will give you the confidence to try new experiences. It will also help you to achieve more, because you will have a positive attitude that makes it easier to deal with setbacks.

Is self-esteem the same as conceit?

No. A conceited person has an exaggerated opinion of themselves. A person with self-esteem has a balanced view of their own worth, valuing their good points, but understanding that like everyone else they are not perfect.

Feeling Confident

Some people seem to be born confident. They can enter a crowded room, immediately feel at home and settle down and talk to anybody. Confidence comes from believing in yourself and feeling happy. Once you're confident about what you want out of life, you can go for it.

When you're confident about yourself – how you look and how you feel – many other problems disappear. Perhaps you have to read some of your work out in front of the whole class. If you feel confident in yourself, you'll be less pre-occupied with things that don't matter – like how you look and where you're sitting – and more concerned with making the reading interesting for the rest of the class.

Know Yourself

Make a list of what your strong points are. You can feel proud of what you're good at.

Not so good points	Good points
tidying room	making friends
getting to sports practice on time	swimming
	telling jokes
handwriting	eating healthy food
cleaning shoes	studying hard
nail biting	organising games
brushing hair	painting
washing dishes	staying fit

Feeling confident will show in the way you look

In pairs

On your own, make one list of the things you are good at, and another list of the things you think you're not so good at. Then show your lists to a partner. Go through the list of good points and discuss the things you've included that make you feel good and that you are most proud of. Then choose one of the things from your not so good list and discuss together something positive that you could do in order to get better at it.

Erica Stewart offers tips on how to build up your self-esteem

1 Think positively

Look at things in a positive rather than a negative way. For example, if you do badly in a test, don't think: 'I'm hopeless. I'm never going to get a good mark.' Instead, think about what you can do to make sure you get a good mark next time, such as asking for extra help with things you don't understand.

2 Stand up for yourself

Make up your own mind about what you believe and stick to it. It's harder to say no than to say yes, but don't let your friends pressurise you into doing things you don't believe are right. Don't feel guilty or that you're letting them down. You'll respect yourself far more for sticking up for your beliefs than if you give in and do something just to please others. And other people will respect you far more, too.

3 Be realistic

Be realistic about what you can achieve. Don't set yourself unachievable targets. If you're really determined to do something, then go for it. But adopt a step-by-step approach, setting yourself a series of short-term goals and dates by which you plan to achieve each one.

4 Cope with criticism

If you're criticised, it can damage your self-esteem. Consider carefully whether the criticism is fair. For example, if you let the rest of the cast down by not turning up for an important play rehearsal, then accept that it was your fault. Apologise and reassure everyone that you won't let it happen again. But if you are being unfairly criticised, recognise what is going on and either ignore it or take steps to ensure that it doesn't continue.

5 Take risks

If you're not prepared to take risks then you cut down on the chances of having new experiences and finding out what you're capable of doing and achieving. Of course, that doesn't mean doing things that are dangerous or reckless. But avoiding taking any risks because you're afraid of making a fool of yourself won't do anything for your self-confidence. It's usually best to have a go. If it doesn't work out, you can always tell yourself that at least you tried.

⊕ In groups

Discuss the advice that Erica Stewart gives in her article. Which piece of advice is the most useful? Which is the hardest to put into practice?

Discuss David's story (below). Talk about how difficult it can be to stand up for yourself. Discuss similar situations in which it can be hard to do what's right for you, because everyone else wants you to do something.

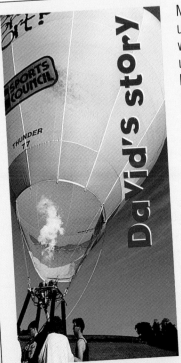

David's story

My friends all wanted to go up in a hot air balloon. So when Ben's father fixed it for us, they all got really excited. But I felt worried, because I'm really scared of heights, and I knew I couldn't face it. Everyone crowded round me, teasing me and calling me all kinds of names. I felt dreadful about it.

Then I put my foot down. I said I wasn't going up, and I didn't care what they thought of me. End of story. Everyone calmed down then, and didn't tease me any more. But I went along on the morning of the flight, and I took some great photographs of the lift-off.

? What do you think?

Study the six statements below. Talk about each one in turn, saying why you agree or disagree with it. Make notes of your views and share them in a class discussion.

1 What other people think of you and your behaviour is more important than what you think yourself.
2 It's not being conceited to feel proud of yourself and your achievements.
3 It's not what you look like that matters, it's what kind of person you are and how you feel about yourself.
4 If you're not confident about doing something, it's better to avoid doing it rather than risk making a fool of yourself.
5 People who keep putting you down only do so to try to make themselves feel better.
6 Imitating people by doing whatever is regarded as cool and trendy is the best way to boost your confidence.

Shyness

Coping with Shyness

Few people are strangers to shyness. It sweeps over us in many situations: arriving at a party, talking in front of the class, starting a conversation with someone important or taking on a new task. Even something as 'simple' as ordering gig tickets over the phone for the first time or signing your name at the bank can make you feel awkward.

Shyness, one of the most complex and untalked about emotions, has many different effects. Dryness of the mouth, fumbling, stuttering, avoiding eye contact, not speaking up, blushing, feeling sick, sweating, headaches: it's no wonder the word most often coupled with shyness is 'crippling'. It can stop you accepting invitations, trying new experiences and getting on in life.

As a teenager you are at the peak of your self-consciousness, and shyness is a result of worrying about your image. You are looking and feeling different, experiencing new emotions and being put in more 'adult' situations, when just a few months before you were being treated like a child. You want to deal with situations smoothly even though you've never encountered them before.

'Adolescents have this image of how they should be coping and it's based on Superman or Superwoman,' says Professor Robert Edelmann, an expert in social anxiety at the Roehampton Institute. 'They want to be seen as confident and competent and it's almost impossible when they're uncomfortable with the way they feel.'

As you become older and more experienced a lot of the awkwardness you feel goes away. But you can help yourself now by recognising that the way you feel reflects your own thoughts. If you're down on yourself – 'No one likes me'; 'I look awful'; 'I don't know what to say' – you're bound to feel shy.

'Awkward situations don't have to be awkward,' advises Professor Edelmann. 'If you stutter or start to dry up, try to make a joke out of it. Say something like, "I just don't know what to say, isn't that weird?" It will change the way people think of you and take away that feeling that it's the end of the world.'

How to beat shyness

● Shy body language can make situations worse. **Try to speak clearly** (mumble and you will be asked to repeat yourself) and look people in the eye.

● **Think positive.** Tell yourself you can cope and you will. Try and focus on what you like about yourself and what you are good at. For example, if you are a good skater, imagine yourself skating confidently.

● **Taking a deep breath** and relaxing will stop your mind working overtime. If your body is calm, you are less likely to fluff your words.

● Shy people are often seen as 'aloof' or 'off' because they stand alone and look unapproachable in social situations. Try to **break the ice** before your anxiety builds up, and don't put on a front.

● **Be realistic.** Just because you are feeling self-conscious doesn't mean everyone is looking at you or analysing your every word. Look at the situation rationally and realise that you are not the centre of attention.

● **Face the fear.** If you are scared of doing something, do it anyway. It's the only way to learn.

⊕ In groups

Discuss what you learn about shyness from the article on this page. Talk about what causes shyness and how it makes you feel.

Discuss the advice that is given on how to cope with shyness. Which do you think are the most useful of the tips?

Coping with classroom mistakes

Being embarrassed and afraid of failing holds girls back from contributing in class. However, not speaking out has far-reaching effects outside the classroom. It can stop you standing up for yourself and your beliefs, and it can make you miss opportunities. If you let the fear of failure (the fear of getting something wrong or saying something embarrassing) overwhelm you at school, it will overwhelm you in everything you do.

The things to remember are:

● It's not the end of the world if you give an incorrect answer.

● Not understanding something isn't a sign of stupidity. Not asking for help is stupid.

● Embarrassment is only momentary.

● No one remembers the things you get wrong.

● Speaking in front of people gets easier the more you do it.

● If someone shouts you down, assert yourself and ask them to let you finish.

Adapted from *Wise Guides: Self Esteem*, by Anita Naik

Making mistakes

Making a mistake can not only be embarrassing, but it can also damage your self-confidence. Everyone makes mistakes.
So when you make a mistake, it's important to keep it in perspective and to learn from it.

Apologising

Learning to say sorry is one of the most mature qualities you can acquire. It's one of those qualities everyone will admire you for because they all know how difficult it is to do. Apologising is not a sign of weakness, so don't look at it that way. In fact, it's just the opposite – it shows you have the confidence to confront a situation and deal with it efficiently. Once you recognise you have made a mistake, try to apologise quickly. Don't make a big deal of it. Get it over with. Feelings of guilt get in the way of other things, and stay on your conscience until they are completely out of proportion. So say sorry as soon as you can. If someone apologises to you, just accept it calmly.

From *Growing Up*

- Learning from your mistakes -

Growing up is all about experiencing things for the first time. It is easy to make a mistake because you are inexperienced.

If you make mistakes because you are careless, try and give more time to things. Take life more slowly. Think things out and plan how you're going to act.

If you think you might make mistakes because you feel uncertain or ignorant about something, talk about it with someone you trust. Don't act without a second opinion.

If you make mistakes because you're nervous, take a deep breath before you act. Don't panic yourself into acting on impulse or in a way which isn't really you, just because you think you must make your mark.

Concentrate on all the good things you can do, and don't dwell on things you aren't so good at. Making mistakes is all about lacking knowledge – and that's something you can work on putting right.

- Don't blame yourself -

If you blame yourself for everything that goes wrong, you'll soon begin to lose confidence in yourself.

But everybody makes mistakes. It's part of human nature. And if you can learn from where you went wrong, you'll become a wiser person.

From *Growing Up*

⊕ In groups

1 Talk about how to cope with classroom mistakes. Is it fair to make fun of people who make mistakes in class?

2 Discuss the advice on learning from your mistakes. What do you think is the most useful piece of advice?

3 Read the statement about apologising. Say why you agree or disagree with it.

for your file

Use the information in this unit as the basis for a short article for a teenage magazine explaining why it is important to have self-esteem and what you can do to build up your self-confidence.

Drugs – Facts and Fictions

66 Many young people who start taking drugs don't realise what they are getting into. There are lots of myths about drugtaking. Before you do anything rash, it's worth knowing all the facts and what risks are involved. 99

– *Drugs counsellor*

Only other people get hooked or hurt by drugs
~~FACT~~ ✓FICTION

Part of the problem with drugs is that most users think they're invincible. They believe that the dangers will never affect them because it's other people who end up being rushed to hospital, other people who can't handle the effects of drugs.

If you're someone who is tempted to take drugs, don't ignore the information and warnings. Drugs can and do kill. They don't discriminate – it could happen to anyone.

People get their drugs from pushers
~~FACT~~ ✓FICTION

Contrary to popular belief, most people come into contact with drugs through friends and older sisters or brothers, not through anonymous pushers on the street. What's more, being approached by someone you like makes saying no harder and more complicated.

All drugs are dangerous
FACT✓ ~~FICTION~~

The danger when taking drugs depends on many things, such as *what* you've taken, *how much* you've taken, and your state of mind at the time. Although some drugs are less dangerous than others, illegally manufactured drugs are *always* a danger because it's impossible to tell what's in them. Never trust a friend who tells you something is safe because they've tried it. Everyone reacts differently to drugs – body size, weight, age and sex all need to be taken into account.

Soft drugs lead to hard drugs
~~FACT~~ ✓FICTION

One of the greatest myths of all time is that taking soft drugs automatically means you'll end up on hard drugs. There is no evidence to suggest that this is true, although taking any kind of drug does increase your chances of coming into contact with harder drugs. This is because drugs like Ecstasy, Speed and LSD are often mixed with other substances, and are often available through the same sources. What you have to remember with drugs is that you always have a choice. A choice not to take them, a choice to stop taking them and a choice not to go any further.

Is *Cannabis* Safe?

You may have heard people say cannabis is risk free. This isn't true.

▶ Heavy use of cannabis over a long period of time can lead to users relying on the drug as a way of relaxing and being sociable.

▶ **Heavy, long-term cannabis use can make you feel less energetic than normal. This can have a negative effect on the way you live your life.**

▶ Smoking cannabis with tobacco causes lung damage. In fact it's reckoned that smoke from an unfiltered spliff carries more risks than a cigarette. However, people tend to smoke many more cigarettes than spliffs.

From The Score: Facts about Drugs

drugs and drugtaking

Name: *The chemical name for ecstasy is MDMA. It has many slang names such as E, echoes and doves.*

Form: *Ecstasy comes as tablets of different shapes, sizes and colours. Because it can look like many other drugs or medicines, a lot of people have been sold tablets which have turned out not to be ecstasy. Since you can never be quite sure what you are buying, a lot of people think buying ecstasy isn't worth the risk.*

Legal category: *Ecstasy is a Class A drug. It is illegal to possess or supply ecstasy.*

Effects: *Ecstasy is a stimulant which users say gives them a 'rush' feeling followed by a sense of calm, making them feel closer to other people and more aware of their surroundings. They get an energy buzz, which means they can dance for long periods. The effects begin about 20 minutes after they've taken a tablet and last for several hours.*

Risks: *As ecstasy starts to work people sometimes feel sick, their heart rate increases and their jaw muscles tighten. Some people become anxious and feel confused and frightened.*

Ecstasy raises the body's temperature. Dancing for a long time in a hot atmosphere after taking ecstasy can lead to overheating and dehydration (loss of too much body fluid). The risks can be reduced by 'chilling out' and taking regular breaks from dancing, and by drinking about a pint of a non-alcoholic fluid, such as water, fruit juice or a sports drink every hour. Users are advised to sip the drink regularly, to avoid alcohol and to eat salty food in order to replace the sodium they have lost through sweating.

Once the effects of the ecstasy wear off, users can feel tired and depressed, but may find it hard to sleep.

Research into the long-term effects of using ecstasy suggest that heavy use may cause damage to the brain, leading to depression and memory loss later in life. Use of ecstasy has also been linked to liver and kidney problems.

There have been at least 60 deaths as a result of taking ecstasy. Evidence suggests that most were as a result of heatstroke.

for your file

Use the information on this page and write an article for a teenage magazine entitled 'Ecstasy – is it worth the risk?' Explain what physical effects ecstasy has – both pleasurable and harmful – and give your views on the risks involved in taking ecstasy.

In groups

What do you learn from these pages about the risks of drugtaking? Discuss the views of these young people (below) and say why you agree or disagree with them.

'Experimenting with drugs is too risky. You don't know what you're taking and how your body will react.'

'There's too much fuss about drugtaking. Most people who take drugs get a good feeling and it doesn't do them any harm.'

'Taking drugs is a waste of money. You don't need drugs in order to have a good time.'

In pairs

Study the article on ecstasy. Make a list of the important facts about ecstasy which you learn from the article.

Role play

Act out a situation in which a doctor explains to a teenager the risks involved in taking ecstasy and smoking cannabis.

Role play a scene in which two people argue about the risks of drugtaking – one saying it's worth the risk, the other saying it's not. Take it in turns to be the person saying it's not worth the risk.

Drugs and the Law

If the police have reason to suspect you're carrying an illegal drug they have the right to make you turn out your pockets. They can also take you to the police station and search you. If drugs are found, you could be charged with one of TWO offences.

1 POSSESSION

This means being caught with an illegal drug for your own use. The police can tell your parents or carer. They could also inform the Social Services and the Probation Service. As for punishment, the police can give you either a reprimand, a warning or prosecute you (see page 39). If you are found guilty in court you can get a fine or a custodial sentence.

2 POSSESSION WITH INTENT TO SUPPLY DRUGS

If you had any intention of dealing (which can include giving and sharing drugs) you may be charged with this more serious offence. Decisions over whether you're charged with intent to supply are based on the circumstances in which you were caught and the quantity of drugs you were caught with. The police can take the same course of action as in simple possession cases, but this time you're more likely to be charged. If your case goes to court the penalties are likely to be heavier.

If you have a drugs record:

Obtaining a visa to travel to some countries may become difficult or could even be denied. It could affect your job prospects. When you're applying for a job, an employer may check if you have a criminal record or any past convictions. *Ignorance won't wash with the law.* The Misuse of Drugs Act divides drugs into three classes and gives guidance for penalties.

Class A

cocaine, crack, ecstasy, heroin, LSD (acid), magic mushrooms prepared for use, speed (amphetamines) if prepared for injection, and in some instances cannabis oil
Maximum Penalties:
   possession: 7 years' prison and/or a fine
   supply: life imprisonment and/or a fine

Class B

cannabis, speed (amphetamines)
Maximum Penalties:
   possession: 5 years' prison and/or a fine
   supply: 14 years' prison and/or a fine

Class C

rohypnol, supply of anabolic steroids and tranquillisers/possession of temazepam (mazzies)
Maximum Penalties:
   possession: 2 years' prison and/or a fine
   supply: 5 years' prison and/or a fine

From *The Score: Facts about Drugs*

⊕ In groups

Discuss what you learn from this page about the laws on drugs.

1 What can the police do if they think you are carrying drugs?

2 What offences could the police charge you with if you are caught carrying drugs?

3 Into what different classes does the law divide illegal drugs? How do the maximum sentences differ according to which class a drug is in?

4 What can be the consequences of having a drugs record?

5 How effective do you think the current drugs laws are? Do you think they act as a deterrent? What effect do you think they have on the way drugtakers obtain and use drugs?

6 Do you think the drugs laws should be changed in any way? Should there be harsher penalties for supplying drugs? What are the arguments for and against making drug use legal and allowing people to possess drugs in small amounts for their own personal use?

for your file

Write a statement giving your views on the drugs laws.

Saying 'no' to drugs

⊕ In groups

Talk about all the different situations in which a teenager might be offered drugs. Why might they choose to refuse or accept? Talk about factors that might influence their decision, such as where they are, who they are with, what mood they are in and how much pressure is put on them to join in.

Discuss the advice which the extract gives on how to turn down drugs and stay friends. Which piece of advice do you think is the most helpful?

↻ Role play

Role play a scene in which a teenager is being offered drugs and a group of their friends is putting pressure on them to accept. Discuss various tactics that the teenager can use in order to say no. Is it best to just say no and walk away? To state clearly the reasons why you personally don't want to take them? To argue with the people who are offering them to you, and try to stop them taking any?

Take it in turns to be the person being pressurised, and discuss which of the tactics worked most successfully.

How to turn down drugs and stay friends

Sometimes saying no just doesn't work. Friends still try to persuade you you're wrong and that you should give drugs a try. It's tough, but you can get round this by not letting yourself be swayed.

I could give you a list of lines to say to help you turn down drugs but, let's face it, you have to say no in your own way or it won't work. This way you'll feel more strongly about what you're saying, and will get your point across in the most confident way possible.

However, remembering the following will help:

▶ No one can make you feel inferior without your consent. Being trendy, cool and mature are all things that come from inside of ourselves and have nothing to do with what we drink, smoke or swallow.

▶ Say no and don't feel bad about it. Obsessing about what you've said, how you've said it, and what people think of you is bad news.

▶ Being the only non drug-taker may feel awkward and uncomfortable but this is just a phase and, like all awkward phases, it will pass.

▶ Don't make things worse for yourself by letting your imagination exaggerate a situation. Being the odd one out is hard but it doesn't mean your friends no longer like you.

❝ When I refused to smoke drugs at a party, I thought all my friends thought I was being stupid. I got so upset about it that I went home early and cried. Over the weekend I decided that if they didn't like me for not taking drugs, I wasn't going to be friends with them any more. When I got to school on Monday, I was all ready to fight with them but then I found out they were all worried about me and had no idea why I'd got so upset. ❞

▶ Strange, but true, no one is judging you. Everyone is so worried about themselves and how they look to other people that they aren't even thinking about you.

▶ Question people who try to bully you into taking drugs. After all, if drugs are so brilliant, why is it so necessary for them to have your company? If someone is giving you grief for saying no, ask them the following:

➡ Why is it so important for you to take them?

➡ Why are they so stressed out about you saying no?

➡ Why do they have to make other people take them too?

From *Wise Guides: Drugs*, by Anita Naik

13

Britain
a multi-cultural society

Today, Britain is a multi-cultural society consisting of people from many different ethnic backgrounds.

The origins of the ethnic diversity in modern Britain lie in the immigration that has taken place from various parts of the world. Many immigrants came to Britain in the years following the end of the Second World War in 1945. During the 1950s and 1960s large numbers of people came to Britain from the Caribbean and from South Asia. Immigration was encouraged during these years because workers were needed to help rebuild the British economy after the war.

In addition to West Indians, Indians, Pakistanis and Bangladeshis, there are important immigrant groups in Britain of Americans, Canadians, Australians, Italians, Greeks, Turkish Cypriots and Chinese.

At the time of the 1991 census, 3,015,051 people living in Britain were not white. This represented 5.5% of the total population. Almost half of these people were born in Britain.

Nearly half of Britain's ethnic population is of Indian, Pakistani or Bangladeshi origin; one-fifth is of Afro-Caribbean origin.

The ethnic composition of Britain (1991 census)

Ethnic group	no.	%
White	51,873,794	94.5
Black Caribbean	499,964	0.9
Black African	212,362	0.4
Black – other	178,401	0.3
Indian	840,255	1.5
Pakistani	476,555	0.9
Bangladeshi	162,835	0.3
Chinese	156,938	0.3
Other Asian	197,534	0.4
Other – other	290,206	0.5
Total ethnic minority population	3,015,051	5.5
Black ethnic groups	890,727	1.6
South Asian	1,479,645	2.1
Chinese and others	644,678	1.2

People from ethnic minorities have introduced their own cultures and lifestyles to Britain. Members of their communities have made significant contributions to society in all walks of life – industry and commerce, medicine and science, politics, the media, arts and sports.

The Joe Bloggs jeans company was founded by Shami Ahmed who came to England from Pakistan when he was two years old

Madhur Jaffrey, the celebrated Indian actress, TV presenter and author of cookery books

Bill Morris, who was elected secretary of the Transport and General Workers' Union in 1992

✛ In groups

Discuss what you learn from this page about ethnic diversity in Britain today.

From Roots of the Future

other cultures and lifestyles

Ethnic stereotyping

It is important not only to respect other people's cultures and lifestyles, but also not to discriminate against them by stereotyping them. **Ethnic stereotyping** means thinking that all people from the same ethnic background have similar characteristics and behave in exactly the same way.

> 66 *I was singing an Asian song with a friend, and my best friend – she's Afro-Caribbean – said, 'Don't tell me you're one of those?' I said to her, 'One of what?' She replied, 'You know, TP,' and I asked her, 'What's TP?' She said, 'Typical Paki.' I answered her, 'So what, I'm proud of what I am.* 99 – Nazrah

> 66 *My friend Asif's a really good footballer. But lots of the other kids say he'll never get anywhere because there's this idea that Asian boys haven't got what it takes to become professional footballers.* 99 – Tariq

⊕ In groups

1 Discuss Nazrah's comment. Are young people from ethnic minorities sometimes stereotyped because of the music they like? Are people sometimes stereotyped because of the way they dress?

2 Discuss Tariq's comment. Then read and discuss John Agard's poem 'Stereotype'. Talk about the stereotypical views that people have of what people from different ethnic groups are good at doing.

3 Talk about national stereotypes, for example, the views that other people sometimes have of English people as either stiff, cold and unfriendly, or as aggressive, beer-drinking football hooligans. What stereotypes are there of **a)** Scottish, **b)** French, **c)** German people? Discuss how these stereotypes have come about and why they present a false image.

Stereotype

I'm a fullblooded
West Indian stereotype
See me straw hat?
Watch it good

I'm a fullblooded
West Indian stereotype
You ask
if I got riddum
in me blood
You going ask!
Man just beat de drum
and don't forget
to pour de rum

I'm a fullblooded
West Indian stereotype
You say
I suppose you can show
us the limbo, can't you?
How you know!
How you know!
You sure

you don't want me
sing you a calypso too
How about that

I'm a fullblooded
West Indian stereotype
You call me
happy-go-lucky
Yes that's me
dressing fancy
and chasing woman
if you think ah lie
bring yuh sister

I'm a fullblooded
West Indian stereotype
You wonder
where do you people
get such riddum
could it be the sunshine
My goodness
just listen to that steelband

Isn't there one thing
you forgot to ask
go on man ask ask
This native will answer anything
How about cricket?
I suppose you're good at it?
Hear this man
good at it!
Put de willow
in me hand
and watch me stripe
de boundary

Yes I'm a fullblooded
West Indian stereotype

that's why I
graduated from Oxford
University
with a degree
in anthropology

John Agard

15

Images and stereotypes

Films and TV programmes

For many years the only way in which black people appeared in Hollywood films was as servants – house cleaners, cooks, gardeners – or in other humble forms of employment. They were never shown as important, powerful or clever people. Nor were they shown as having an individual personality.

The Chinese – in fact most people from Asia – were also only seen in certain stereotypical roles. They were portrayed as untrustworthy, cruel, pathetically over-polite, or associated with opium dens. In these ways certain ethnic groups come to be seen only in crude caricature, like cartoon characters. Their existence, as real people with real lives and real

Spike Lee

The Cosby Show

feelings and thoughts, became invisible.

The cinema has been a hugely popular medium of entertainment, and images presented in film can influence very large numbers of people.

In the United States the stereotypes of black people have changed but often still remain stereotypes. Nowadays you don't see the old 'Southern' image of the black female cook, for example, but you do see the stereotype of the black male criminal. Many black actors, producers and film directors are increasingly aware of this and are improving matters by pushing for appropriate images of black people in films and on TV. Some of the all-black TV soaps, for example, do a lot to present a more varied, normal range of black characters, not just the old stereotypes. The Cosby Show in the USA not only countered racial stereotypes, it also succeeded in gaining audiences of viewers that were larger than almost all other TV shows. Black film directors, such as Spike Lee, often fight hard in their films to tackle the issue of racism directly.

✛ In groups

1 Discuss what is meant by **negative stereotyping** and how films used to present negative stereotypes of people from ethnic minorities.

2 Study the article from *The Guardian* newspaper. Do you agree with the views expressed by the people who were interviewed, that TV programmes do not reflect the multi-cultural nature of society?

3 Talk about recent TV programmes and films which have featured people from ethnic minorities. Discuss how the characters were portrayed and whether or not you think they were stereotypes.

4 Choose a popular TV soap, and share ideas for introducing two new characters from an ethnic minority background. Discuss how you would integrate them into the story in order to present a true picture of what life is like for people from their background in Britain today.

TV 'failing to reflect multi-cultural society'

Television is lagging behind society and failing to reflect the multicultural nature of the country, says a report. Viewers from minority ethnic groups feel that programmes are guilty of presenting characters from ethnic minorities as two-dimensional and without a role in society as a whole.

Those interviewed for the Broadcasting Standards Commission report, Include Me In, were concerned that characters were included to make a point rather than play an integral part in the drama.

Negative stereotyping was still evident, the report found, with several people mentioning a particular episode of Coronation Street in which a black character was introduced, only to become involved immediately in a crime.

Other characters, such as the former EastEnders couple Gita and Sanjay Kapoor, were distinctive only for their skin colour, and did not represent any of the concerns or issues facing Asian families, the survey found.

One interviewee said: 'Gita and Sanjay are Asians, but they don't show any religious ceremonies or relatives and stuff like that. What's the point of having ethnic minorities and not portraying them in an honest way?'

From The Guardian, 8 December 1999

A distorted picture

'White British people have a picture of India as just dirty. The India they see on telly, it's all dirty, with women in rags. It's not all like that but that's all they show. They show the bad parts of India, not any of the good. Bombay, you get a completely different image of that city from the films they make there. I'm sure a lot of it is idealized and that it's not like in the films, but at least that's an alternative picture.

Another aspect of the problem is the way they show Indian people, whether here or in India. A recent example was about

A derilict area in Calcutta

an incident in Kent. The first item on the news was about the election. I'm not saying that's unimportant, but it was nothing central, just a politician visiting a factory or something like that. Then they showed a fight in Kent, an item about Sikhs, and it was only on for about two or three seconds near the end of the news. No information was given about the background, or explanation of the situation between Sikhs and other religions in India, so you can imagine the impression people would have got about Sikhs. Violent. Nothing else is shown about the Sikh community so people get their image from this one incident.'

An internet café in Bangalore

Satnam

From Speaking Out – Black Girls in Britain, by Audrey Osler

News reports

✚ In groups

Discuss what Satnam says about how British people can get a false impression of India and of Sikhs from the way they are presented in the press.

Study some recent editions of either a national newspaper or a local newspaper. Discuss the reports and articles they carry about people from ethnic minorities. What images of them do they convey? Do they present a true picture of what their lives are like and the contribution they make to society?

for your file

What do you think newspapers should be doing to make sure that they do not reinforce stereotyping? Write a letter either to a national or local newspaper saying what you think the editor and staff should be doing to make sure that they do not stereotype people in their paper.

The Press

What people read in the newspapers can also influence how they think about other social groups, including ethnic and 'racial' minorities. If, for example, people from India are always presented as poor, starving or the victims of drought, that creates a false picture of Indians in general, even though it is right to report the human tragedies. Newspaper readers may never get to hear about the Indian scientists, writers, entrepreneurs, film-makers, artists, engineers and so on, not to mention the everyday, normal lives of normal people.

Only joking?

✚ In groups

'Most people who enjoy racist jokes think that jokes are not important. But many jokes depend on stereotypes, and racist jokes reinforce racist stereotypes.'

Talk about how certain comedians use stereotyping as a cheap way of getting laughs. Discuss how such stereotyping is based not only on people's behaviour and appearance but on the way they speak (their accents) and the language they use (their dialect).

What is your view of racial jokes – are they harmful or harmless?

You and your money – gambling

Gambling – the lure and the law

Gambling is one of the country's favourite leisure activities. Every week millions of people buy a ticket for the National Lottery and watch the draw on television. Other popular forms of gambling are betting on horse races, doing the football pools and going to bingo. About two-thirds of over 18s place bets on major horse races.

Officially, the law does not allow children to gamble. But many children do. Surveys suggest that 3 million young people in the UK gamble.

Why do young people gamble?

❝ *It's glamorous. You see people in films and on TV gambling and you want to be like them.* ❞

❝ *It's fun. It gives you something to do when you're bored.* ❞

❝ *It's exciting. You're taking a risk and it gives you a real buzz waiting to see if you've won.* ❞

❝ *It's a way of escaping from the real world and all your problems.* ❞

❝ *The people I know who gamble do it because they can't stop themselves. They're addicted.* ❞

❝ *People gamble to try and win lots of money to make their dreams come true.* ❞

Gambling and the law

There are tight legal restrictions on gambling. The laws are designed to enable people who choose to gamble to enjoy the pleasure of gambling, and at the same time to protect them from being cheated or exploited. For example, all fruit machines are required by law to return a minimum of 71 per cent of the stake money in prizes.

Young people are protected by making it illegal for them to gamble until they are considered old enough to gamble responsibly. The law says that you are not allowed to take part in most forms of gambling until you are 18. But you can do the football pools or buy a National Lottery ticket when you are 16, and you can play fruit machines with a token/cash payout at any age.

⊕ In groups

'It's too easy for young people to gamble. There should be tighter controls.' Do you agree?

Discuss why gambling is condemned in some religions. Make a list of all the moral and religious arguments against gambling you can think of, and say why you agree or disagree with them.

for your file

Write a statement saying what you think are the reasons why people gamble, what your attitude to gambling is and whether you think the gambling laws should be changed.

Winners and losers

A very few people who gamble win huge amounts of money, but most people who gamble lose their money. Because so many people gamble, the gambling industry is big business, with a vast daily turnover of more than £110 million.

The winners in the gambling industry are the people who make profits from the money that is gambled – for example, the pools companies and the bookmakers.

The other big winner is the government which receives over £1.7 billion a year in taxes on gambling.

Fruit Machine Facts

1. About 65% of teenagers play fruit machines. Of these, roughly 6% will become addicted to them.

2. Although fruit machines require a low cash input to start with, the rate the machines play at means money is used up very quickly. At least £3 is spent by addicts on each machine.

3. There's no skill at all involved in playing fruit machines, just as there's no surefire way to beat the system. Far more money goes into the machine than is paid out.

4. Never think of a fruit machine as an easy way to make money. You may have a couple of big wins when you begin playing, but don't let this fool you into putting more money in. Regardless of how many times you get lucky, you're in a no-win situation.

5. If you think you have a problem with fruit machines, speak to your parents. You may need professional help to break the habit. Don't forget you can always call Childline on 0800 1111.

From *Shout*, issue 127 © D.C. Thomson & Co. Ltd

The National Lottery

Since its introduction in November 1994, the National Lottery has proved a huge success. By June 2000 the total ticket sales had reached £28 billion.

The success of the National Lottery means that billions of pounds have been distributed to 'good causes', such as sports and arts projects, funded by the National Lotteries charities board. Also, as a direct result of the lottery tens of thousands of new jobs have been created.

However, many charities reported that there was a significant fall in the amount of donations they received, following the introduction of the lottery. Critics also argue that it is wrong for the lottery to be run as a profit-making venture and that the licence to run the lottery in future should go to a non-profit-making organisation. They also say that the introduction of the lottery has led to the creation of a gambling culture, in which more people are interested in and addicted to gambling. In particular, it encourages lots of the poorest members of society to spend money they cannot afford on lottery tickets rather than essentials, such as food and clothing.

3p Running costs
1p Camelot / 13p Government
50p Prizes
28p Good causes
5p Retailers

Where each pound spent on a lottery ticket goes

✛ In groups

Talk about the National Lottery. What do you think of the criticisms that are made about the way it is run and the influence that it has had? Do you think introducing the National Lottery was a good idea? Do you think any changes should be made to the National Lottery? Give reasons for your views.

Teenage gambling

'Gambling has taken over my life!'

Two young people tell how gambling has affected their lives.

Keri (14) spends all her money on scratchcards, even though she's legally too young to buy them …

❝ The first time I bought a scratchcard I felt really nervous. But my friends were all doing it, and I didn't want to be the odd one out. I was sure the shopkeeper would know we were under-age. But he didn't say anything. We probably got away with it because we all look a bit older than we really are.

I only had a pound on me and I didn't win anything. But one of my friends did and I couldn't wait to have another go. I went back the next day and I won a tenner. It gave me such a great feeling. I bought a few more, but I didn't win again that day.

Then the following week, I had another win. I began to think I must be one of those people born lucky. Especially as none of my friends were winning. They began to lose interest and started saying it was a mug's game.

But the more cards I bought, the more convinced I became that one day I'd buy the one that would win me the jackpot. It got so that I couldn't walk past a newsagent's without wanting to go in and buy a scratchcard.

I love the thrill as you see the numbers being revealed and I'm just waiting for the day when I have that big win. I get some money for babysitting at weekends and it all goes on scratchcards.

Once I even took some money out of my mum's purse. I know I shouldn't have done, but I was going to put it back when I won. Only that day I lost.

My best friend keeps telling me that I'm obsessed. We fell out yesterday because she says I'm boring. She says I've never got any money to do anything and all I think about is scratchcards. I'm frightened I'm going to lose her friendship. But it's got so I don't think I can live without doing them. ❞

Jason is 15 and addicted to arcade machines. He's stolen things from his home and sold them to fund his habit …

❝ When I was 12 I started to hang round with this older boy, Kev. He took me down the arcades and taught me how to play the machines. I found it really exciting, especially the noise and the lights flashing when you won.

Before I knew it I was hooked. I couldn't wait to get down the arcade. I started skipping school to go there and I'd spend all my dinner money and pocket money on the machines.

I was so desperate for money that I raided my savings and when they ran out I started to sell my things. I even stole my sister's personal stereo and sold it to get money for the machines.

The breaking point came when I started shoplifting. Of course, I got caught and when my parents found out they went berserk.

But they've been really supportive. They've made me realise that I'm addicted to gambling in the way that some people get addicted to drugs. Stopping going down the arcade to play the machines has been really difficult. I've suffered from withdrawal symptoms. I go to see this counsellor and he's really helpful. He's made me face up to the fact that I've got a problem. ❞

⊕ In groups

Discuss the effect that gambling has had on Keri's life and Jason's life. Talk about why some people get addicted to buying scratchcards or playing arcade machines.

Problem gambling

Experts consider that a person has a problem with gambling when:

✦ They are unable to stop gambling whether they are winning or losing.
✦ The urge to gamble overrides all other considerations.
✦ They are psychologically dependent on gambling because they experience a 'high' when they are gambling.

If you think a friend has a gambling problem, you can help them by:

1 Letting them know by saying you think they may have a problem.

2 Suggesting that they need to be honest with themselves and others.

3 Encouraging them to talk to their parents and/or a trusted adult.

Who can help?

✦ GamCare, Suite 1 Catherine House, 25–27 Catherine Place, Westminster, London SW1E 6DU
✦ National Gambling Helpline, 0845 6000 133

From A Certain Ref

Responsible Gambling

Gambling can quickly get out of control and create serious problems with money, relationships and other aspects of your life. In order to prevent problems occurring, when you gamble remember the following points:

☆ **You are buying entertainment – not investing your money.**
☆ Before playing, set strict limits on how much time and money you are going to spend.
☆ **Quit when you are ahead.**
☆ Only gamble with money you can afford to lose.
☆ **Do not 'chase' your losses.**
☆ Keep up your other interests and hobbies to ensure your gambling does not take over.
☆ **Gambling in moderation is okay and 'healthy'.**
☆ The key is to gamble responsibly.

From Gambling: A Guide for Young People

⟳ Role play

Role play the following scenes:

1 A group of friends are discussing what to do. Two of them want to go to an amusement arcade to play the machines and try to put pressure on the other two to go with them. Take it in turns to be the two who don't want to go, and discuss ways of saying no firmly.

2 A gang of friends are planning to pool their money to buy some scratchcards and to share any winnings. One of the friends is against the idea and thinks they'd get more value for money if they went to the swimming pool or the fairground instead. Take it in turns to be the 'odd one out'.

✚ In groups

Discuss these statements and say whether you agree with them:

❝ *Only people who haven't got enough to do waste their time and money gambling.* ❞
❝ *Gambling creates more hardship and misery than it gives pleasure.* ❞

for your file

Write an article for a magazine for young people about teenage gambling, describing the problems that it can cause and offering advice on how to gamble responsibly.

5 You and your values –

What influences how you behave?

The way you behave is influenced by what your beliefs and values are. For example, in some situations your behaviour might depend on how important you think it is to impress people, compared to doing what you believe to be right.

What plays the most important part in influencing how you behave? Here are some possibilities. On your own, rank them in level of importance on a five-point scale – 1 for extremely important, 5 for not at all important.

Trying to avoid arguments

Standing up for what you believe is right

Making sure your actions don't hurt other people

Trying to impress people

Listening to what your parents and teachers say

Keeping out of trouble

Doing what your religion says you should do

Keeping your temper

Following the latest fashion

Behaving with courtesy

Telling the truth

Looking after your own interests

Imitating the behaviour of your idols

Respecting other people's opinions and beliefs

Keeping your promises

Doing what your friends want you to do

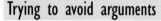In groups

Compare how you have ranked the things that influence your behaviour and discuss what you think the most important influences should be.

Your ambitions

What you believe to be important, and what your values are, will influence your ambitions.

Here is what a group of young people said when asked what their ambitions were:

" To make money. "

" To get married. "

" To have a satisfying career. "

" To live a long life. "

" To contribute to the community. "

" To have people's respect. "

" To travel the world. "

" To become famous. "

" To make the most of my talents. "

" To have children. "

" To help other people. "

" To be happy. "

" To keep fit and healthy. "

In groups

Study the list of things which young people said were important to them when asked to think about their ambitions. Add anything else to the list which you think is important. Then each list what are the five most important things to you personally and talk about why they are important to you.

Heroes and idols

 In groups

Discuss what Derek Stuart says in his article about the difference between idols and heroes. Do you agree with him? What do you think is the difference between an idol and a hero? Together decide what your definition of a hero is.

Draw up a list of people you consider to be heroes who your group would put in their 'hall of fame'. Draft a short statement explaining your reasons for including each person. Then present your views in a class discussion and agree on a class list of our top twenty heroes.

Someone I admire

Think of someone you know personally and admire for some reason, perhaps because of what they have achieved, the way they behave towards other people or the courage and determination they have shown in difficult circumstances. It could be a relative, a friend of the family or a neighbour.

Study the list of qualities (below) and pick out the qualities which make you admire them:

> **intelligence   tact   courage
> determination   unselfishness
> tolerance   cheerfulness   patience
> generosity   loyalty   reliability
> kindness   sympathy   creativity**

In pairs

Take it in turns to tell each other about the person you admire and why you admire them.

IDOLS OR HEROES?

by Derek Stuart

Everyone has famous people that they look up to and admire, but are they idols or heroes?

Many teenagers when asked who they admire most give the name of a film star, a pop singer, a TV celebrity or a sports star. These people certainly have talent and are often good-looking. Many of them have worked hard and shown determination to achieve what they have. They are rich and famous and have exciting lifestyles. But are they really heroes?

The way I see it, a hero is somebody who has shown exceptional qualities. They are people like Nelson Mandela, who was prepared to go to prison to fight for his rights. They are people who are prepared to risk or sacrifice their lives for other people. They are people who achieve things against the odds and who set an example to us all by the way they behave.

So when I'm drawing up my list of heroes for my hall of fame, I'm looking beyond the stars of stage and screen, playing field and catwalk to those exceptional human beings whose behaviour has been truly heroic.

Cause for concern

The ten reports on these two pages all appeared in newspapers during the same week. Which of the issues raised in the reports do you think is the most important?

A

Moves to relax the laws on cannabis

By David Taylor — Home Affairs Editor

A MAJOR inquiry into Britain's drugs laws, backed by Prince Charles, will call for moves towards the decriminalisation of cannabis.

The study will also say the Government should admit Ecstasy is a "soft" relatively harmless drug and no longer a Class A substance alongside heroin and cocaine.

Today's edition of The Economist discloses that the Prince's Trust-funded investigation by the Police Foundation calls for significant relaxation of some drug laws.

The report, out this spring, is certain to provoke controversy.

From The Express, 14 January 2000

B

Pay-out for man denied bar job over his ponytail

By Paul Stokes

A MAN who was denied a part-time job because his hair was in a ponytail has been awarded more than £500 by an industrial tribunal.

Mark Pell, 21 today, claimed he was a victim of sexual discrimination by Neil Wagstaff, a pub manager.

He was told that he would not be considered for the two-nights-a-week job unless he had it cut.

The tribunal in Sheffield awarded £566.69 for injury to feelings and loss of wages. It said the pub's code on long hair was "outmoded".

Mr Wagstaff, 46, said yesterday that the award was ridiculous. "This is political correctness gone overboard."

From The Express, 14 January 2000

C

Blair to support police on stop laws

Eben Black   Chief Political Correspondent

CONTROVERSIAL stop-and-search powers for the police will be backed by the prime minister this week as an important weapon in the fight against crime.

The laws, which allow police to stop and detain anyone they suspect of having committed a crime, were at the centre of a renewed debate earlier this month after Neville Lawrence, father of the murdered black teenager Stephen, was stopped by police looking for a robbery suspect.

Ethnic minority groups say the laws are used disproportionately against them, particularly against black youths. The number of such incidents in the Metropolitan police area has been falling because of the furore.

But Tony Blair, in a meeting this week with the incoming Metropolitan police commissioner, Sir John Stevens, will give his personal backing to stop and search, his spokesman said yesterday. He will repeat the message to rank-and-file policemen with an article in the Metropolitan police staff magazine, The Job.

From Sunday Times, 16 January 2000

D

Short wants overseas aid reform Bill

By Jon Hibbs, Political Correspondent

CLARE Short is fighting a Cabinet battle for legislation in the next session of Parliament to confirm her campaign to end world poverty.

The International Development Secretary wants her reforms to overseas aid enshrined into law, making it harder for a future government to reverse them.

Officials in her department have been ordered to draft plans for the first International Development Act in more than 20 years.

It is intended to underpin Labour's manifesto pledge to reverse the decline in overseas aid, which fell to 0.27 per cent of national income under the Tories.

The United Nations target is 0.7 per cent of gross domestic product.

Miss Short also wants legislation to confirm the abolition of discredited aid and trade provisions, under which development assistance was linked to contracts.

However, she still has to persuade the Cabinet to make room for it in what could be the last full parliamentary session before an election.

From The Daily Telegraph, 6 January 2000

E

Straw backs down over boxer for the money-makers

By John Chapman

MIKE Tyson will be allowed into Britain despite his conviction for rape, Home Secretary Jack Straw ruled last night.

The boxer's sell-out fight with Julius Francis will now go ahead in Manchester later this month as planned. Tyson, once the most feared heavyweight in the world, is due to arrive on Concorde on Sunday.

Promoters had feared that he would be barred by immigration officials at Heathrow. But Mr Straw said he had decided to let him in because of the potentially devastating effect on British businesses which were depending on profits from the fight.

Some small firms could face bankruptcy because they had invested heavily in the contest, he said. "I have also taken account of the inconvenience and disappointment of the many thousand members of the public who had purchased tickets in good faith."

From The Express, 14 January 2000

'Dolly' man to clone herd of 1,500 cows

Jonathan Leake   Science Editor

SCIENTISTS are building the world's first clone farm. A researcher from the Roslin Institute in Edinburgh, which created Dolly the sheep, has moved to New Zealand to help build up a 1,500-strong herd of genetically engineered cows.

The cows, intended to produce medicines in their milk, will mark the first attempt to use cloning in commercial agriculture. Eventually clone farms could be set up throughout the world to help combat diseases including multiple sclerosis and cystic fibrosis.

Many New Zealanders are outraged by the project which they have dubbed "Frankenstein's farm". They say that it and another scheme for a 10,000-strong flock of "transgenic" sheep will destroy New Zealand's reputation for being free of genetic engineering.

From Sunday Times, 9 January 2000

From The Guardian, 7 January 2000

GM ban is extended by Tesco

Tesco has banned its fresh fruit and vegetable suppliers from growing food on sites used previously for trials of genetically modified crops.

The supermarket chain said yesterday that it needed to be able to assure customers no GM material has come into contact with its produce. Its decision was welcomed by eco-campaigners Greenpeace, but criticised by the government for being a marketing ploy.

Other supermarkets may consider following Tesco's lead, but it remains to be seen whether farmers are deterred from volunteering for trials of GM oilseed rape, beet and maize; most involved so far are cereal producers.

Tesco has already pledged not to stock any GM crops, and is also trying to ensure that all feed for animals that supply its meats is GM free.

Get on your bikes and cut the traffic jams, pupils are urged

BY JOHN INGHAM   ENVIRONMENT EDITOR

BIKE sheds and buses were yesterday unveiled as the answer to the traffic jams caused by the school run.

A Government panel called for cheap bus travel for all schoolchildren and better, more secure bicycle facilities at schools.

The School Travel Advisory Group also wants local authorities to introduce school buses for children not entitled to free fares and the Highway Code and driving tests to include sections on school travel. The committee would like to double the number of children travelling to school under their own steam within ten years.

This would take children back to traffic levels recorded in the mid-1980s. But ultimately the panel hopes to "make it possible for every child to walk, cycle or take the bus or train to school". It claims that this will bring long-term health benefits to the children and unclog congested roads.

The plans were criticised for not going far enough and for failing to tackle the safety issue. Many parents fear their children will be run over or attacked by perverts if left to make their own way to school.

From The Express, 14 January 2000

---

25 species that could vanish

TWENTY-FIVE species of primates are in danger of extinction, a report revealed yesterday. "As we enter the new millennium we risk losing our closest living relatives in the animal kingdom," said Russell Mittermeier, president of Conservation International.

The group blames the destruction of habitat, attacks by hunters and the capture of animals for the pet trade or medical research. The most endangered primates include the golden bamboo lemur in Madagascar, the yellow-tailed woolly monkey in the tropical Andes and the mountain gorilla (right) in central Africa.

From The Express, 12 January 2000

Owners of airguns face curbs

AIRGUN users could be forced to get a licence under a future Firearms Bill, a Home Office minister revealed yesterday. Charles Clarke said this was one of several new restrictions being considered and that all-embracing legislation was seen as the "ideal way" to rationalise the gun laws.

He told the home affairs committee inquiring into controls on firearms that the apparent increase in the use of airguns was not a "healthy development". Figures showed that the annual number of airgun offences went up from 5,172 in 1987 to 7,506 in 1997.

From The Daily Telegraph, 12 January 2000

---

for your file

Choose one of the issues on which you have a strong opinion and write a letter expressing your views on the issue.

Cut out a newspaper report which raises an issue that you feel strongly about. Put it in your file and write a comment saying why you have chosen that particular report.

◖◗ In pairs

Study the reports and then list them in order of what you consider to be the importance of the issues they raise. For example, if you think D is the most important write down 1 – D and so on.

⊞ In groups

Compare your lists. Talk about why you consider some issues to be more important than others.

Imagine your group is the editorial committee of a weekly TV news programme in which topical issues are discussed. Decide which four issues you would include in the programme. Then role play a discussion about one of the issues.

Separation and divorce

From Girls Know Best, edited by Michelle Roehm

Dealing with divorce

Marie (14), Ellen (12) and Laura (10) have watched their parents get divorced. They talk about what they have learned from their experience.

Why do people get divorced?

Laura: Because they don't like each other as much as they did before.

Ellen: They are changing or have changed.

Marie: Each situation is unique and has its own set of reasons. Most reasons are too complicated and adult-related for parents to share with their children. That's good. There are some things we really don't need to know. Don't be afraid to say that to a parent who is telling you things about the other parent that you think are none of your business (but say it nicely!).

I'm scared about my parents' divorce. What can I do?

Laura: It's okay to be scared. I was scared when my parents got divorced. Just hang on in there!

Ellen: Your parents aren't spending as much time with you and they might be cranky. That doesn't mean they don't love you. They need some space and some time.

Marie: Of course, you're scared – it's a scary thing. Think about why you are scared. Let your parents know what you are thinking. They can reassure you. They're scared too, but you can all support each other.

Can I make my parents get back together?

Laura: No, and don't try. If they stay together, they won't be happy and they'll probably just fight.

Ellen: No. Lots of kids probably try, but it won't work, so don't get involved doing something that will just frustrate everyone.

Marie: Just like us, our parents have to choose their own paths. You can't do anything that will get them back together. It's their problem and their job to make life work for themselves. The decision to divorce is probably not something they made in a hurry. They've likely thought about all of the possibilities and they see this as the best thing to do.

Is it my fault that my parents are getting divorced?

Laura: No. How could it be? They're the grown-ups, you're just a kid.

Ellen: No. This is between your parents. There's nothing a kid could do that would cause a divorce.

⊕ In groups

Discuss what Marie, Ellen and Laura say about parents divorcing, and say whether or not you agree with them.

List all the different reasons you can think of why relationships between parents break up. Is it none of your business, or do you think children have a right to an explanation when their parents decide to split up? Does it depend on how old you are?

⑦ What do you think?

In groups, study each of the eight statements below. On your own write down whether you agree with it (A), disagree with it (D) or are not sure (N/S). Then compare your views in a group discussion.

1 It's better for parents to split up than to stay together for their children's sake.

2 Splitting up is an easy option. Too many parents take the easy way out.

3 Children should never take one parent's side.

4 It's better for parents to split up than to spend all the time arguing and quarrelling.

5 Parents should involve children in discussions about splitting up.

6 A one-parent family can never be as happy as a two-parent family.

7 Parents who split up are selfish. They're only thinking of themselves.

8 Children are bound to suffer when parents split up.

divided families

A mixture of feelings

Children often experience a mixture of feelings when their parents separate.

Whatever you feel, it's important to recognise your feelings and not to bottle them up. Talking can help. So find someone you can trust and talk to them honestly.

. . . .

Who decides who you live with?

In the majority of divorce cases, it's your parents who will decide which of them you are going to live with. They will also agree the arrangements for you to see your other parent. But if they are unable to agree, then the court will decide.

The court will take your views into consideration as well as those of your parents. The court may make two orders – a **residence order** and a **contact order**.

A residence order states which person you are going to live with. A contact order specifies the arrangements for you to see your absent parent. A typical arrangement is that you will spend alternate weekends with them and a week with them at Christmas, Easter and in the summer.

In pairs

'Children should always have the final say in deciding who they are going to live with.' Discuss this view.

Shock
" I just couldn't believe it. I felt totally numb. I went round in a kind of daze. It wasn't until my grandma talked to me that I realised I'd been suffering from shock." Nathan (14)

Anger
" I was furious with them both. I started taking it out on everybody and everything. I played truant from school and even got in trouble with the police. Of course, that just made things worse. " Darrell (15)

Sadness
" I felt so unhappy. I just couldn't stop crying. We'd been such a happy family and now it was all over. " Heather (13)

Guilt
" I got myself into a right state. I was convinced that I must be to blame. " Alanna (14)

Relief
" To be honest, it was a relief. The tension had become so unbearable that I'd dread going home to find them fighting again. Now there was an end in sight. " Mitchell (16)

Insecurity
" I felt frightened and insecure. I didn't know what was going to happen to me. Would we have enough money? Would I have to change schools? What would my friends think? " Kirsten (14)

for your file

Study Pat's letter (below) and write an answer to it.

My parents are separating and I feel it's all my fault. Whenever they argue it seems to be about me. Mum says Dad's too hard on me and he says I'm selfish and spoilt. I feel desperate. I'd do anything to help keep them together. I couldn't bear it if they split up. – Pat

Coping with change

When your parents separate there can be major changes in your life. You may have to move home or school. The parent you live with may be short of money. You may find it hard to keep contact with the absent parent. You may find it difficult when the parent you live with starts to form a new relationship.

⊕ In groups

Read the stories on this page and talk about the changes that these people had to face when their parents separated.

1 Talk about what it feels like to become part of a one-parent family after being in a two-parent family. How typical do you think Barbara's experience is?

2 Discuss Chris's problem and say what you think he should do about it.

3 Talk about what Xanthe says. Do you think her experience is unusual? Explain why.

A quarter of all teenagers whose parents divorce lose contact with the absent parent after two years. Discuss why you think this happens. How important do you think it is to try to keep in contact with both your parents after a divorce? Is it always desirable, whatever the circumstances? Give reasons for your views.

◖ In pairs

Many children find it difficult to tell their friends and other people that their parents are separating. Discuss why they find it hard. Is it better to be upfront about it and to tell everybody, or do you think it's your family's business and that there's no need to tell anyone if you don't feel like it?

We had to move to a small flat

Barbara lived in a large house before her parents split up, but it has now been sold and Barbara is living in a small flat with her mother.

'It's not nearly as nice as our old place. She says it's only until she can get on her feet, and then we'll get a better place.

Also, she has to work full-time now. She's always tired – she comes in, does a few jobs around the flat and then collapses in front of the TV. I don't think she's got a very well-paid job, so I know there's not going to be much money for a while. I'm going to get a part-time job as soon as I'm old enough to buy clothes and things for myself.'

From Dealing with Family Break-Up, by Kate Haycock

I want to be with my mates

Chris found that it was a problem pleasing both his father and himself. He felt really guilty because he was bored when he was with his dad.

'I spend every weekend with my dad. We really get on and I know he enjoys my visits. The trouble is, I end up feeling really bored. Dad makes me feel guilty because on a Saturday night I want to go out with my mates, not sit at home and watch TV, however much he likes having me around.'

From Caught in the Middle, by M. & Susan Jackson

I get the best of both worlds

Some young people, like Xanthe, speak positively of an arrangement where they split their time between two parents.

'I actually enjoyed seeing my parents separately. We often used to find it difficult to agree on things, but now I do different things with my mum and with my dad. They make more of an effort to do things with me, like taking me ice-skating or to the cinema, and I make less of a fuss when they ask me to help out with chores and things like that. I feel I get the best of both worlds.

I also spend more time with each of them on their own, and have got closer to them and know them better as people. Now that we have adjusted to life after the break-up, I actually prefer it like this to how it was before.'

From Dealing with Family Break-Up, by Kate Haycock

How to cope with step-parents

Living in a stepfamily

❝ *I hated my stepmum, Sharon, but now I know her better, I think she's really sweet and nice. We disagree sometimes and she aggravates me a lot, but she's OK really.* ❞
Janet (14)

❝ *When I visited dad, it was fun having a stepbrother to do things with, but my father wasn't there for me. He showed favouritism to my stepbrother. He spent more time with him than me. I really felt pushed into the background.* ❞
Jason (16)

❝ *I was gob-smacked when Mum told us she was pregnant. So were my stepbrothers. We were pretty mean to Mum during her pregnancy. Amazingly when Pete was born, it brought us together because he belonged to both families.* ❞ Rachel (16)

 In groups

What do you learn from the statements above about the problems children face when settling in to a stepfamily? What other problems and difficulties might stepchildren face?

Study the article (right). Which do you think is the most useful piece of advice **a)** on how to cope with step-parents; **b)** on how to get on with stepbrothers and stepsisters?

If you're going to be living with your step-parents, don't expect everything to be brilliant from the start. Everyone will have a lot of adjusting to do, and just getting used to each other's habits is a big step.

Your step-parent isn't a substitute for your real mum or dad. But that doesn't mean you can't form a close, loving relationship with him or her. Why not give it a chance?

If you do have problems with a step-parent, it can help to talk to someone who isn't closely involved, maybe a friend or a teacher you get on with. Often someone a bit more distant from the problem can stand back, take a good look and suggest things that might help.

Try to get to know your stepmum or dad as a person, not just see them as a threat. Until you actually find out a bit about him or her and discover what their personality's like, how do you know you aren't going to get on?

If you really are having big problems with a step-parent, try having a private word with your mum or dad about it. They're still your mum or dad and will want to sort things out.

Brothers and sisters

Adjusting to having a stepbrother or stepsister also takes time. If you're having problems, think of the following:

All families are different. So if, for example, you're used to having a lie-in at weekends and your stepbrothers and sisters like to get up at the crack of dawn and watch TV with the sound up high, you'll need to reach a compromise. Of course, that means talking about how you feel – not shouting!

If you do argue, it's not the end of the world. After all, real brothers and sisters argue all the time, so it's only natural to argue with your new brothers and sisters, isn't it?

Try to see stepbrothers and sisters as potential friends. If you both make an effort, you can end up close and good mates – much better than being at war with them!

Respect their space and privacy. Even if you have to share a room, work out a few ground rules between you so there aren't any misunderstandings.

Your mum or dad remarrying definitely takes a lot of getting used to and can be a very upsetting time. But if everyone makes the effort, you should end up as a happy family – it just takes a bit of effort and a lot of compromise all round.

Adapted from *Shout*, issue 118 © D.C. Thomson & Co. Ltd

for your file

A friend called Jan is very upset because her mother is getting remarried. She is feeling resentful and anxious about moving in with her stepfather and his two children. She thinks she will have to share a bedroom. Write a letter offering Jan advice on how to cope with the new situation.

Safety at home

Every year thousands of people are injured in accidents at home. You need to know what to do in an emergency. The commonest type of accidents are falls.

✚ What to do if someone falls

> Even if you think a bone is broken, do not move the person if the injury looks serious. This is particularly important if you think the neck or spine is injured because damage to the spinal cord can cause permanent paralysis.
> Go and call an ambulance.
> Keep the person warm.
> Do not give the injured person anything to drink in case they need to be given an anaesthetic later.

✚ First aid for fractures

Sometimes it may be difficult to tell for certain whether a bone is broken. Signs are as follows:
> pain and tenderness at the point of injury;
> swelling;
> deformity or unusual shape;
> loss of movement.

Do not move the casualty until you have immobilised the fracture, which means making sure it cannot move. Movement of the broken ends can cause more damage, pain and shock. If it is a broken leg, immobilise it by putting some soft padding between the legs and tying the injured leg gently but firmly to the other leg at the ankles and knees. If it is a broken arm, immobilise it by putting the casualty's arm across the chest and supporting it with an arm sling.

✚ First aid for cuts

If you lose too much blood your body won't get enough oxygen. Severe bleeding can cause death, so the first thing you must do is stop the bleeding. Put your thumb and/or fingers on the wound and press firmly. If it is a large cut, try pressing the edges together. Keep pressing until the bleeding stops. This may take up to 15 minutes.

If direct pressure won't stop the bleeding, press gently but firmly above and below the wound. If you can, raise the injured part so that it is above the level of the casualty's chest. This slows down the blood flow from the heart to the injured part.

A large cut which won't stop bleeding or which has gaping edges may need stitches. Don't try to clean it or to take out any object embedded in the wound. Removing it could cause more damage and might increase the bleeding, since the object may be plugging the wound. Bandage the wound with a clean dressing and get medical help.

If it is a small cut or a graze, clean the wound with soap and water, then dry it and put on a sterile dressing or an adhesive plaster. The size of the pad touching the wound must always be larger than the wound. Don't use any creams or ointments. They do not help and may delay healing by making the skin soggy.

◑ In pairs

Study the information on this page, then write answers to these questions.

1 What signs and symptoms may indicate that a casualty might have a fractured leg?

2 Explain the first aid treatment that you would give someone you suspect has **a)** a broken leg, **b)** a broken arm.

3 If someone is bleeding badly, why is it dangerous? How would you try to stop the bleeding?

4 How would you treat **a)** a wound with an object embedded in it, **b)** a grazed knee?

for your file

Find out what you should do if someone is suffocating or choking, then write out a set of first aid instructions. Call them 'What to do if someone is suffocating' and 'What to do if someone is choking'.

✚ First aid for burns and scalds

When you get a burn or a scald, it damages your skin and destroys the blood vessels just below the surface. The first aid treatment is the same for burns and scalds.

1. Pour water over the burn at once. This reduces the heat in the skin.

2. Keep putting on cold water for at least ten minutes. Either hold the burn under a cold tap or dip it into a bowl or a bath of cold water.

3. Burnt skin often swells up. Take off anything near the burn which may be tight, such as a ring, a bracelet or a watch.

4. Cover the burn with a clean dry dressing from your first aid box or use a cotton pillow case or a linen tea towel. This will help to protect the skin from the risk of infection.

5. If the person is badly burned, call an ambulance.

6. Don't try to pull off any clothes that are stuck to the skin. Don't put any cream or ointment on the burn or use a fluffy cloth to cover the burn.

◖◗ In pairs

Discuss how scalding accidents can occur **a)** in the kitchen, **b)** in the bathroom. What steps can you take to try to prevent them occurring?

🔄 Role play

Imagine one of you was baby-sitting when a young child got burned. Tell a friend how you gave the child first aid.

What to do if the house is on fire

1 Get everyone out of the house as fast as possible. Lots of deaths in fires are caused by people breathing in fumes and suffocating. So don't stay in the house and try to put the fire out.

2 Call the fire brigade by dialling 999 (see page 36). Don't just think that someone else will already have done so.

3 If you have time, close all doors and windows. This can stop the fire spreading, because it reduces draughts which may fan the flames.

If someone's clothes are on fire ...

▲ Pull the person to the ground. This stops the fire from spreading upwards towards the face.

▲ Grab a coat, rug or blanket and use it to smother the flames. But don't use anything made of nylon, because nylon shrivels and melts in heat.

Many potential fire hazards are found in people's homes

Chip pans

Many kitchen fires are caused by chip pans catching fire, often because the pan is too full. If a chip pan catches fire, switch the cooker off, cover the pan with a lid or damp cloth and leave it to cool down. Do not take it off the cooker and put it under the cold tap.

for your file

Design a poster *either* to tell people how to protect their homes from fire *or* to tell them what action to take in an emergency if a house catches fire or if someone is burned.

What is child abuse?

Abuse occurs when adults hurt children or young people under 18, either physically or in some other way. Usually the adult is someone the child or young person knows well, such as a parent, relative or friend of the family.

But Nina's got a new pair! It's not fair!

*Not getting your own way all the time is **not** an example of child abuse.*

Corinne Pearlman

There are four main kinds of abuse:

PHYSICAL ABUSE includes hitting, kicking and punching, and may even lead to death.

EMOTIONAL ABUSE includes sarcasm, degrading punishments, threats and not giving love and affection, which can undermine a young person's confidence.

NEGLECT occurs when basic needs, such as food, warmth and medical care, are not met. Being thrown out of home may also be an example of neglect.

SEXUAL ABUSE occurs if an adult pressurises or forces a young person to take part in any kind of sexual activity. This can include kissing, touching the young person's genitals or breasts, intercourse or oral sex. If an adult asks you to touch his or her genitals, or to look at pornographic magazines or videos, these are examples of sexual abuse.

As well as causing suffering at the time, there may be long-term difficulties for young people who have been abused. All forms of abuse are wrong and have damaging effects on children and young people.

Why does it happen?

No one knows exactly why some adults take advantage of their position of authority over young people in this way. There may be many different reasons. Stress, money problems, unhappy circumstances, the feeling of having no power in adult relationships, and having been abused as a child may all play a part. But it is hard to predict with certainty which factors cause an adult to abuse a child.

Some adults may even convince themselves that there is nothing wrong with their behaviour, or that it is for the child's own good.

But whatever the reason, abuse is **always** wrong and it is **never** the young person's fault.

⊕ In groups

'A good hiding never did anyone any harm.' Say why you agree or disagree with this view.

FACTS and FICTIONS about ABUSE

1 When a young person is abused, the offender is more likely to be a stranger. **FALSE** – *In the majority of reported cases the offender is someone the young person knows.*

2 Girls are more at risk of abuse than boys. **FALSE** – *Boys are at risk almost as much as girls, though boys report abuse less.*

3 The majority of offences of abuse are carried out by men. **TRUE** – *Most reported cases of abuse are by men.*

4 Victims are sometimes to blame for the abuse because of the way they behaved. **FALSE** – *It is never the victim's fault, no matter how they behaved. It is always the abuser's fault.*

5 If anyone attempts to touch you in a way that makes you feel uncomfortable, you have the right to tell them not to do so. **TRUE** – *It is your body and you have the right to decide who touches you and who doesn't.*

From Speaking Out About Abuse

Sexual abuse

I feel so guilty and ashamed

There was this friend of my dad's who I got on really well with. One evening he came round while my parents were out and put this video on which showed people having sex. He sat down beside me and put his arm round me and started touching me all over. I tried to tell him to stop but he wouldn't listen and made me touch him. He told me that what we were doing was all right and it was to be our secret. I've never told anyone about it before, because I feel so guilty and ashamed about what happened.

Kayleigh

Adapted from *Sussed and Streetwise*, by Jane Goldman

If you are being abused, it is extremely important to understand that *you* haven't done anything wrong. The victim is *never* to blame for what happens to them, and yet so many victims of abuse feel guilty. No one deserves to be abused, and no matter how you react in a situation where you're being abused (whether you don't put up a fight, whether you maybe even experience sexual feelings that aren't entirely unpleasant) you are not responsible for what happened to you. If you have feelings of guilt, try to fight them, because you have *nothing* to feel guilty about. Concentrate on feeling angry with your abuser instead, and determined to protect yourself and put things right.

The most important thing to do if you have been abused is to tell someone about it. Choose a responsible adult who you trust. If you're afraid to tell a parent or guardian (perhaps because the abuser is someone close to them), choose another older relative, a teacher you like or your doctor. If you can't think of anyone you'd feel comfortable talking to, or you think you might prefer to talk to someone you don't know, you can get help and advice by ringing a helpline.

NSPCC Child Protection Helpline: this is a free 24-hour service, which you can ring either if you think you are being abused yourself, or if you are worried about a friend. Telephone: 0800 800 500.

Childline: this is a helpline for young people who are in trouble or danger. You can also contact them if you are concerned about a friend being abused. Telephone: 0800 1111.

What happens next?

When you tell an adult about serious abuse, he or she may have to involve other people to help you sort things out. Usually there will be a social worker, and sometimes a police officer and doctor. What happens next is called an **investigation**. In order to help you, these professionals will ask you questions to find out exactly what happened. These questions may be embarrassing or difficult. But the adults involved are used to talking to young people who have had similar experiences, and should make it as easy as possible for you. As part of the investigation, the professionals will probably also speak to your family and other people who know you well. After the investigation there may be a **case conference** where the professionals will meet and make decisions about how best to help you. You might be able to go along to all or part of the case conference.

During the investigation and case conference, it is important that you make sure that the professionals know how *you* feel. Try not to be afraid to ask questions, and let them know how they could make things easier for you.

Young people who have been abused are only taken away from home if it is felt that it is dangerous for them to stay. The majority stay in their own home. Most of those who are removed return home just as soon as it is felt that they will be safe.

Saying no

 Role play

If an adult starts pressurising you to do something you don't want to do, tell them firmly to stop.

With your partner, take it in turns to practise saying no. Role play a scene in which a friend is putting pressure on you to do something that is reckless or dangerous. Practise saying no politely but firmly.

From *Speaking Out About Abuse*

33

Safety in the street

We would all like to be able to walk through the streets alone without feeling frightened, and we all have a right to be able to feel safe whatever we do. Unfortunately, sometimes that is not always possible so it is important to know what we can do to make sure that we stay safe.

Staying safe in the street.........

* Keep to main, well-lit paths.
* Don't walk closely behind people who are walking alone.
* Don't accept unorganised lifts.
* Invest in a personal alarm.
* Walk facing the traffic. Think about the clothes you are wearing if you have to walk home late at night. For example, trousers are better than tight skirts.
* If attacked shout FIRE – not 'rape' or 'help', as more people are likely to respond.
* Carry enough change to be able to make a phone call.
* Be aware of your surroundings – especially at a cash point, telephone booth, near pubs and clubs.
* Tell someone where you are going and when you will be back.

Safety on buses.................

* If you're waiting at a quiet bus stop at night, look to see if there's a café or shop that you can wait inside till your bus comes.
* At night don't go upstairs on a double-decker. Try to find an aisle seat and sit near the driver.
* Don't travel alone if you can avoid doing so.
* If you feel threatened go and stand close to the driver and tell them why you are doing so.
* If you are getting off alone at a quiet stop, arrange for someone to meet you there.

Adapted from Respect: Your Life Your Choice

What should you do if …

⊕ In groups

Discuss what you think a person should do in each of these situations.

1 You are travelling home on the bus late at night and a stranger comes and sits next to you and starts to chat you up.

2 You are walking along the street and a car pulls up alongside and the people inside offer you a lift.

3 You are travelling on a crowded bus and you feel someone stroking your thigh.

4 You are walking through a shopping precinct and you get the feeling that someone is following you.

5 You are in a lift and someone gets in who makes you feel uncomfortable.

6 You are walking past a group of people and they start shouting insults and making lewd comments.

7 You enter the hallway of the block of flats where you live and you see someone hanging about that you don't like the look of.

8 You are in a video arcade and a man offers to pay for some games for you because he says he likes to help young people out.

9 You are walking home with a friend who suggests that you take a short cut that will save you twenty minutes but it means going down a lonely lane.

10 The person who said they'd drive you home has taken drugs or got drunk and you've no money to get yourself home.

Safety in public places

If you like to hang around in parks, on the beach, in arcades, fast food places, shopping precincts, or any other public place, take these precautions:

■ Stay with your friends, or at least within sight of them.
■ Avoid these places at night, especially if they are deserted or tend to attract gangs.
■ Avoid deserted toilets. Go with a friend.

Keep an eye out for lone adults, especially men or older boys, who hang about where young people congregate. If he tries to make friends with you, or he offers you money, food, drink or drugs, refuse and act cold or distant. If he persists or you see him playing a lot with a particular child, tell the shopkeepers in the arcade, your parents or another trusted adult about him.

If you want to go for a long walk in the park or in the country by yourself, think about how safe you'll feel and what you could do if you were attacked. How near would you be to houses or streets where you could get help? Do you know your way out of the park, or your way home? No amount of self-defence awareness should make you feel that you can't enjoy the countryside. But at the same time you should be cautious. If your local park is known to be unsafe at certain hours, don't go in at those times. If you go off on a walk, make sure someone knows where you are going and when you expect to be back.

If someone talks to you persistently

'I was stuck on a train once during a breakdown, and this middle-aged man started chatting to me. I didn't like him because he was pushy, so I acted cold and moved away from him. He got the message, but then he turned to this other teenage girl and started talking to her. She was too embarrassed to be rude to him, and pretty soon he was touching her earrings and necklace and asking her about her boyfriends and making her blush. She looked embarrassed because everyone could hear.'

Don't let someone intimidate you into putting up with pushy, personal, or unpleasant conversation. If he's insensitive enough to keep bothering you, you don't have to worry about being rude to him. If brief, cold answers and a turned-away head don't stop him, pointedly moving away from him should. If you are absolutely stuck next to him in a rush-hour crowd, shout, 'There's a man bothering me here, please let me through.' Make sure he's the one who is embarrassed, not you.

The Golden Rule of Self-Defence

The golden rule of self-defence is to pay attention to and trust your instincts. Countless victims of sexual assault and other crimes have said, 'I felt something was wrong, but I didn't want to look stupid, so I didn't do anything.' If you feel uncomfortable around a person or a place, if a warning signal goes off somewhere deep inside you, if you feel scared or just uneasy, don't ignore it. It is always better to act on your warning instincts and never know whether you were right than to ignore them and find yourself a victim; a moment of looking foolish is nothing compared to being assaulted.

From *Stand Up For Yourself*, by Helen Benedict

In groups

Plan a short video for young people designed to tell them how to stay safe in the street. First, decide exactly what tips you want your video to give, then discuss how you are going to put your messages across. Draft a detailed plan for your video, then choose someone to explain it to the rest of the class and share your ideas in a class discussion.

for your file

Design a leaflet for young people called 'Safety in the Street – How to Protect Yourself Outside'.

Safety on the road

Every year thousands of young people are injured on the roads. There is more risk of a cyclist having a road accident than any other road user except a motorcyclist.

Cycling Safely

You are most at risk on a bicycle when you are either turning right, going round a roundabout, crossing the pavement or riding at night.

Turning right

When you're turning right, look behind you for traffic. If it's clear, give an arm signal early. Then move towards the centre of the road to take up the correct position for turning. Repeat the arm signal and give a last 'life-saver' look over your right shoulder before turning.

At roundabouts

You have to give way to traffic coming from the right. It is usually safer to stay in the left-hand lane all the way round. But you need to watch out for vehicles wanting to cross your path to leave the roundabout.

Crossing the pavement

Lots of accidents are caused by children riding across the pavement and straight out into the road. You should wheel your bicycle across the pavement and then wait for a gap in the traffic.

At night

Riding at night is dangerous because it can be difficult for drivers to see you. It is against the law to ride without lights and a reflector. It is also a good idea to wear something bright which reflects in a car's headlights. Another thing you can do is to fix reflectors on the pedals.

From *English Direct* 1, by John Foster and Keith West

Design a comic strip or write a cautionary tale about a young person who gets hurt in a cycling accident because they weren't cycling safely.

In groups

1 The most dangerous age for cyclists is 12 to 14, and five times as many boys get hurt as girls. Discuss why.

2 List the various ways of carrying things on a bicycle. Which are the safest ways and why?

3 'It should be illegal to ride a bicycle when you're not wearing a safety helmet.' Say why you agree or disagree with this view.

4 Draw up a list of 'Dos' and 'Don'ts' for cyclists. Compare your list with the 'Extra Rules for Cyclists' in the Highway Code.

5 How often should you check your bicycle? Which parts should you check? Draft a bicycle maintenance checklist.

6 Prepare an outline for a TV advert designed to make young people of your age aware of the dangers of riding recklessly.

How to make an emergency telephone call

In an emergency find a telephone and call for help. You don't need money to pay for the call.

1 Lift the receiver and press or dial 999.

2 Tell the operator which emergency service you want:
Fire, Police or Ambulance.

3 Wait for the operator to connect you to the Emergency Service.

4 Tell the Emergency Service:
WHERE the trouble is,
WHAT the trouble is,
WHERE you are and the number of the phone you are using.

NEVER make a false call. You could risk the lives of others who really need help and it's against the law.

Emergency first aid

When you are faced with an emergency, do not rush in immediately with first aid. Pause to assess the situation first. Look around to make sure that you are not going to endanger yourself or the casualty. You must then decide how the injury should be treated.

Shock

A person who has had a serious injury, severe pain or serious loss of blood may be suffering from the condition called shock. The symptoms of shock vary depending on how serious the condition is. The symptoms include paleness, feeling faint, cold and clammy skin, a weak and fast pulse, fast and shallow breathing. Shock can cause unconsciousness and even death. The aim of first aid for shock is to prevent the shock from getting worse.

1 Get the casualty to lie down and deal with any injuries.

2 If the casualty has lost a lot of blood, keep the head down and if possible raise the lower limbs. But do not do this if you think there may be a head injury or that a leg may be broken.

3 Cover the casualty with a blanket, rug or coat to keep him or her warm, but not too hot.

4 Do not give anything to drink in case the person needs to have an anaesthetic when she/he gets to hospital.

Unconsciousness

1 Check that the person is breathing properly. Make sure there are no obstructions in the mouth. Remove any false teeth, chewing gum or vomit.

2 Stop any severe bleeding by pressing firmly on the wound.

3 If the person stops breathing, give mouth-to-mouth resuscitation.

4 It can be dangerous for an unconscious person to lie on her or his back, because the tongue may fall back and block the airway. Once you are sure that breathing is satisfactory and any severe bleeding is controlled you should put the person in the recovery position (see diagram). This prevents the tongue from falling back and allows any blood, fluid or vomit to drain out of the mouth.

5 It can be dangerous to move someone who has broken bones or internal injuries. Do not move such a casualty unless you have to do so because there is further danger, such as from traffic or fire.

6 Do not leave an unconscious person alone unless you have to because there is no one else around and you need to fetch help.

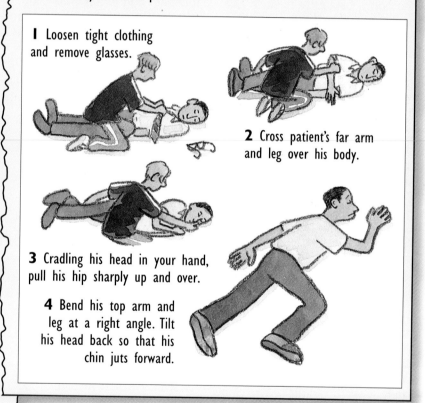

1 Loosen tight clothing and remove glasses.

2 Cross patient's far arm and leg over his body.

3 Cradling his head in your hand, pull his hip sharply up and over.

4 Bend his top arm and leg at a right angle. Tilt his head back so that his chin juts forward.

In pairs

Draw up a list of 'Dos' and 'Don'ts' when giving emergency first aid to an unconscious person.

Discuss what shock is, what the symptoms are and how it should be treated.

Practise putting each other into the recovery position.

Police duties and police powers

The duties of the police force are:

1 To protect life and property.

2 To maintain public order.

3 To prevent and detect crime.

The police couldn't do anything at all without help from the general public, and most of their information comes from what people tell them. To do their job, the police obviously need to ask people questions and search their property. A lot of the law which sets out police duties and powers is contained in the Police and Criminal Evidence Act 1984.

— Stopping —

If a police officer stops you in the street, you are entitled to know the officer's name and the police station where he or she works. You are also entitled to know why the officer has stopped you. It is not acceptable for this to be simply because of your colour, dress, hairstyle or the fact that you might have been in trouble before.

You don't strictly have to answer an officer's questions, unless he or she suspects that you have committed (or are about to commit) an arrestable offence – such as theft, assault or carrying an offensive weapon. In these circumstances you must give your name and address, but need not answer any more questions.

REMEMBER If you're stopped by the police, keep calm and don't overreact. If you're obstructive and rude, you're more likely to be arrested. Staying calm will also help you remember what happened and what was said. Don't deliberately mislead the police by giving false information or wasting their time.

— Searching —

The police do not have the power to search anyone they choose. You cannot be forced to be searched unless you have been arrested or are suspected of carrying:

✗ drugs

✗ stolen goods

✗ weapons, or anything that might be used as a weapon

✗ anything that might be used for burglary or theft.

If you are searched, the officer should explain why the search is taking place and what he or she expects to find.

Any search which involves more than a check of your outer clothing should be done out of public view or in a police station or van. If the search requires more than the removal of outer clothing, it should be done by someone of the same sex.

REMEMBER Stay calm, and make sure you know why you're being searched. If the police search you illegally, they are committing an assault, but if they have good reason, and you refuse, you may be charged with obstruction.

⊕ In groups

1 What do you learn from this page about police powers to stop and search you in the street?

2 Discuss the views on stop and search (below). Which do you agree with and why? Where appropriate, support your views by giving examples from your own experience.

❝ *The police have too much power to interfere in our lives. The police powers of stop and search are an infringement of our liberty to move around freely.* ❞

❝ *If the police didn't have the powers to stop and search people it would be even easier for criminals to break the law and get away with it.* ❞

Helping the police

If you are asked to go to a police station to help with enquiries it's important to know whether you are being arrested. If you are being asked to go voluntarily, you may refuse – although the police may then decide to arrest you – and then you have to go.

If you are at the police station you are entitled to send a message to your family or a friend telling them where you are, and also to free legal advice from a solicitor. If you have not been arrested, you may leave at any time you wish.

Questioning

If you are 16 or under you should never be interviewed without your parent or an appropriate adult (such as a teacher or social worker) being present. However, you should also have a solicitor present to advise you. You must give the police your name and address, but you have the right not to answer any further questions.

Reprimands, Warnings and Prosecutions

If you have broken the law, whether you will receive a reprimand or a warning or are prosecuted will depend on the offence, whether you admit it and how many offences you have committed.

There are now limits on how many 'last chances' the police can give you before you end up in court. If you commit a really serious offence you will be prosecuted straight away. If you commit a less serious offence, the police can give you a maximum of only two chances before you will definitely be taken to court.

As soon as you break the law, even for something you might consider minor (like dropping litter or riding a bicycle on the pavement) the police will give you a reprimand for the first time and a warning for the second time. If you break the law for a third time you will automatically be sent to court and prosecuted.

If you are given a reprimand, the police officer talks to you about what you have done and explains what will happen to you if you break the law again. They will remind you about who you have hurt by breaking the law – your family as well as your victim. The police will keep a record of your crime. You may find that your details are passed on to a Youth Offending Team who will decide if any further action should be taken.

If you are given a warning, the police will talk to you and put your crimes on record in the same way as for a reprimand. You are automatically referred to a Youth Offending Team who will generally decide what type of scheme to put you on to stop you committing any more crimes.

Reprimands and warnings can only be given to people who have admitted that they have broken the law. This means that someone who has committed an offence and does not admit it cannot be given a reprimand or warning. In these cases they will be sent to court and prosecuted.

Prosecution means your case will be heard in the youth court. If the court finds you guilty, you will be sentenced. You will then have a criminal conviction.

What records are kept on young offenders?

If the police reprimand you, warn you or charge you with a recordable offence, they will take your fingerprints and a photograph of you. These records, and a written description of you and the offence you committed, will be added to the files on the Police National Computer.

If you are 10 or 11 years old, the records on you will stay 'live' on the Police National Computer until your 17th birthday. If you are older, the records will stay active for five years.

From *Youth Justice*

⊕ In groups

Discuss what you learn from this page about the system for dealing with young people who break the law. Do you think it is fair always to prosecute a person for their third offence, however minor their first two offences might have been? Give reasons for your views.

Keeping the peace

A lot of police time is spent controlling large crowds. As well as looking after crowds at football matches and other sporting events, the police also supervise demonstrations and public protest meetings. Every year the Metropolitan Police deals with several hundred demonstrations and processions in central London.

The police attend demonstrations and disputes to make sure that the law is not broken, and to protect both sides. Many demonstrations are carried out peacefully and no incidents occur. Occasionally, though, violence breaks out and the police have to act to protect people and property.

Sometimes the police are accused of causing trouble by the way they treat demonstrators. From reports you have read in the newspapers or seen on television, do you think there is any evidence that the police cause trouble at demonstrations?

❝ *The police might have been on duty at a demonstration for hours. Then you have just one flare-up as one small group gets out of hand. A few helmets roll in a scuffle, and a couple of demonstrators get dragged to a police van. It makes good television, just right for the introduction to the news bulletin, but it gives a totally false picture of what has been going on. We know for a fact that television cameras and their spotlights egg a crowd on.* ❞ – Senior police officer

⊕ In groups

Discuss times when you have been in a large crowd that the police have been controlling. Talk about the way the police handled the crowd and any incidents that occurred. What do you think of the way the police controlled the crowd?

Discuss what the senior police officer said. Do you think television often presents a distorted picture of what happens at demonstrations?

RAVES

Many raves are legal and are organised in conjunction with the local licensing authorities. Organisers need an entertainment licence and to get this they must meet certain safety standards. Illegal raves, however, are unlicensed – and often without adequate safety precautions. These are more likely to be dangerous, particularly if there is overcrowding.

Under the Criminal Justice and Public Order Act 1994 the police have the power to break up an unlicensed open-air rave of more than 100 people if it seems that the noise and disturbance are likely to cause distress to the local inhabitants. This means that under the orders of a senior police officer, the police can order from the land anyone who is preparing, waiting for, or attending a rave.

From *Young Citizen's Passport: Your Guide to the Law*

Doing a good job?

What do you think of the police?

❓ What do you think?

What is your attitude towards the police? On your own, study each of the statements (below) and decide whether you agree with it, disagree with it or are not sure. Then share your views in a class discussion.

1 People don't respect the police as much as they should.
2 You can rely on the police to help you if you are in trouble.
3 Many police officers are dishonest and untrustworthy.
4 The police are friendly and polite.
5 The police are good at catching criminals and maintaining law and order.
6 The police are racist and treat white people better than black people and Asians.
7 The police have a difficult job to do and they do it as well as they can.
8 The police are bullies and misuse their authority.
9 Teenagers don't like the police because the police don't like teenagers.
10 TV programmes about the police give a false picture of how the police behave.
11 The police interfere in our lives too much.
12 The media only report the mistakes the police make, not all the good things they do.

for your file

Write a short statement saying what you think of the way the police behave and what your attitude to the police is.

It is easy to see the police as a nuisance, or even as the enemy, but they are just doing a job which can save lives and try to make our society a better place. There will be times in your life when that particular sentiment will seem tragic but believe it or not the police are helping to protect you, so help them and help yourselves.

Police regulation ▼▼▼▼▼▼▼▼▼▼

Contrary to popular belief, the police are not above the law. They follow the law, just like us, and are also regulated by a separate set of guidelines. These are outlined in the Police and Criminal Evidence Act 1984 and you can get hold of a copy at your local library or police station.

An officer has broken the disciplinary code that the police must follow if he or she:

▼ neglects his or her duty;

▼ makes a false statement, written or spoken;

▼ misuses his or her authority;

▼ is abusive to a member of the public;

▼ is racially discriminant in any way.

You can make an official complaint if you think an officer has broken this code. Before you do, get legal advice from a solicitor – you can see one free of charge at your local Citizens Advice Bureau.

From Teen Law

Making friends

In pairs

Discuss the list of statements about friends and friendships. Decide whether you think each statement is **a)** true, **b)** sometimes true, **c)** not true. Make a note of your views, then join up with another pair and share your views in a group discussion.

The secret of making friends

Anita Naik offers advice on how to make and keep friends

Be patient and sensitive

No matter how much you like someone, don't demand too much, too soon; it may freak the other person out. No one likes to be pushed into things, nor to feel suffocated by another's attentions. Chill out, and let the relationship grow naturally.

Listen to your own conscience

If a prospective friend does something that makes you feel uncomfortable, don't be afraid to break off. Likewise, if someone makes you feel bad about yourself, then dump them – they're no good for you. So that bad feelings aren't left to ferment and therefore cloud whatever remains of the friendship, be up front and let them know what's bugging you.

Learn to be trusting

It's impossible to have a friendship if there is no element of trust. Both people have to be open, honest and not afraid to say no.

Be forgiving

Some people just can't cut it in the friendship stakes; they may let you down, stand you up, or blab something that was meant to be just between the two of you. What you've got to do is understand the limits of particular friendships.

You must not think that one disappointing friendship means that they'll all be disappointing. Learn to understand and forgive your friends their shortcomings. There will be some people who will always be there for you, and there will be others who won't.

It's okay to have lots of friends

Without being at all disloyal, you can have different friends for different things. Some mates are ice-skating buddies, others are school pals and others you see only once a week at dance class. To some friends you will be an open book and they will know all your deepest, darkest fears. Other friends will only know the barest details. That's fine. Don't get worked up about making every friend a best friend.

What is a friend?

1. A friend must share your interests.
2. A friend is someone you can trust.
3. A friend should have a similar personality to you.
4. A friend should share your values.
5. A friend should always cover up for you.
6. A friend is someone who you can tell your private thoughts and feelings.
7. A friend is someone who won't tease you.
8. A friend must be approved of by your parents.
9. A friend is someone who won't disagree with you.
10. A friend is someone who will forgive you.

In groups

Do you agree with what Anita Naik says about how to make and keep friends?

Make lists of **a)** the kinds of behaviour that help to cement a friendship, **b)** the kinds of behaviour that are likely to destroy a friendship.

for your file

Write your views on friends and friendships. Say how important friendships are to you, what you value most in a friendship and what your expectations of friendships are.

From *Friends and Enemies*, by Anita Naik

friends and friendships

Problems with friendships

Growing ← → Apart

'We used to do everything together. But lately she's become very offhand and all she seems interested in is boys. Quite frankly, I now find her boring a lot of the time I'm with her. But when she doesn't come round like she used to, then I miss her.'

Gemma

Most friendships start because the two people involved have lots in common, so when one of you grows up faster than the other and finds new interests it can change everything between you. If that happens, it's sad, but often the only thing to do is to have a bit of a break from being best friends and each see other friends who share your interests.

If you and your friends are growing apart ...

Don't ✗

* make the situation into a big row so you end up falling out forever and making yourself even more unhappy. OK, so you don't have much in common with each other just now — but maybe in a few months you'll find one or both of you has changed and you might just want to be mates again! Give each other a bit of space, but try to keep in touch.

* blame yourself. This hasn't happened because you're a terrible friend or there's something wrong with you — it's simply that people change.

* feel bad if you're the one who feels you're growing out of your old mates. It's not like you're doing it on purpose and it happens to lots of people — it's all part of growing up.

Do ✓

* see this as an opportunity to make new mates rather than fretting too much about the past. If you're the one who's feeling dumped it's easy to wallow in self-pity and lose your confidence, but look at it this way — now you're free to find mates who you really have things in common with.

* remember that you won't be the only one going through this. It's easy to imagine everyone else is paired off already and won't want you, but if you look closer you'll probably see other mates are going through sticky patches over exactly the same kind of problem.

* confide in someone at home about what's going on so you can get a bit of extra support while you're making some new friends.

From *Shout*, Summer Special
1999 © D.C. Thomson & Co. Ltd

The Rules of Friendship

1. Keep secrets.
2. Wait for your friend to offer secrets; do not pry.
3. Share your happy times as well as your sad times.
4. Stand up for your friends.
5. Show loving support.
6. Ask your friends for support when you need help.
7. Offer help; do not just wait for your friend to ask.
8. Make sure you return borrowed things.
9. If your friend hurts your feelings, say so. Don't go off in a sulk.
10. Look in your friend's eyes when you talk.
11. Don't joke about or tease your friend.
12. Don't be jealous of your friend's other relationships.

From Play Stay Keep Safe

⊕ In groups

Study 'The rules of friendship'. Discuss whether you agree or disagree with each one. Are there any other rules you would add to the list? Which three rules do you think are the most important?

Study the article from *Shout* (left). Discuss the advice that it gives on how to deal with the situation if a friend is growing apart from you.

How much are you influenced by your friends?

How do you behave when you're with your friends? Do you let your friends influence your decisions, or do you always make up your own mind and do what you think is right? Do this quiz to find out how much you let your friends influence you. Keep a record of your answers, and then check what your answers tell you about your behaviour when you are with your friends.

1 **You are with a friend** and they say something you do not agree with. *Do you…*

a agree with them to avoid an argument;

b only say what you think if they ask your opinion;

c tell them you don't agree with them and explain why?

2 **Some friends dare** you to do something reckless that could have serious consequences. *Do you…*

a agree to do it in order to try to impress them;

b find an excuse for not doing it;

c refuse and say you're not prepared to be so reckless?

3 **A group of your friends** are teasing someone and making hurtful remarks about them. *Do you…*

a join in because they expect you to do so;

b not join in, but do nothing to stop them;

c try to get them to stop?

4 **You have become friends with** someone none of the rest of your friends like. *Do you…*

a drop your new friend;

b ask your friends why they don't like your new friend then decide what to do;

c tell them that it's none of their business and you'll be friends with who you choose?

5 **Your friends ask you to do something** that may get you into trouble with the police. *Do you…*

a join in because everyone else is;

b try and persuade them it's wrong, but go along with them if they won't listen;

c tell them you're not joining in and walk away?

6 **Two of your friends have a row and** fall out. *Do you…*

a take the side of the person you like best;

b leave them to sort it out and try not to get involved;

c listen to both sides and support whoever you think is in the right?

7 **One of your friends asks you to tell a** lie to stop them getting into trouble with their parents. *Do you…*

a agree to do so because you are afraid of losing their friendship;

b say you'll only do so if you are not covering up anything serious;

c say no and explain that you can't get involved in what's going on between them and their parents?

8 **Your friends are talking about sex in** a way that you don't like. *Do you…*

a join in, even though you feel uncomfortable;

b keep quiet, but not show your disapproval;

c tell them why you don't like the way they are talking?

What do your answers tell you? See next page

What your answers tell you about how much you are influenced by your friends

Mostly 'a's You are so concerned about what your friends think of you that you will do almost anything to keep in with them. You're allowing them to influence you so much that you've stopped thinking for yourself. You need to listen far more to what your instincts and conscience tell you about how to behave than to think about what will most impress your friends. You must start asserting yourself and acting according to your beliefs rather than just doing things to please others.

Mostly 'b's You hesitate before saying or doing things that you don't believe in, and sometimes you allow yourself to do things that you don't want to do in order not to upset your friends. When faced with an awkward situation you tend to look for the easy way out. You need to start trusting your own judgement more and to be more prepared to speak out and do things that might set you apart from the crowd.

Mostly 'c's You have a healthy disregard for what others might think of you and are prepared to stand up for yourself and do what you believe is right. Sometimes it will cause difficulties with friends, but you understand that it is more important to stick to your principles rather than to do things just to curry favour. Your actions give you self-respect because you don't allow people to pressurise you, and those people who are your friends know where they stand with you and can rely on you to speak your mind.

 In pairs

Talk about what you have learned from this activity about how much influence you let your friends have on you.

Role play

Role play a series of situations in which one friend puts pressure on another to do something they do not want to do. The person who is being pressurised refuses firmly but politely and explains their reasons. Take it in turns to be the person saying 'No'.

One of you asks the other: **a)** to spread a false rumour about someone in the class who they don't like; **b)** to tell their parents that they spent the evening at your house; **c)** to look after a package for them for a few days; **d)** to go truanting with them; **e)** to go somewhere your parents have forbidden you to go.

for your file

Write a story about someone who allows a friend to pressurise them into doing something which they later regret.

Gangs

❝ *I used to be part of a gang. But they made me do things I didn't want to do and I got into trouble. Now I steer clear of them.* ❞

❝ *Belonging to a gang is great. You really feel you're somebody. We do all kinds of crazy things together. It's a great laugh.* ❞

❝ *I think people who go round in gangs are weak. They give each other courage to do things they're too cowardly to do on their own.* ❞

In groups

Study the article 'Gangs – Know the Facts' (right). Why do people go round in gangs? Discuss the way people behave in gangs. Talk about your experiences of gangs and say what you think of the way gangs treat their members and people who aren't members.

Gangs – Know the Facts

💀 A gang is not simply a group of friends who hang around together. Gangs intimidate people.

💀 Gangs rule by fear, and this doesn't just apply to the people they pick on. Often, gang members get involved in trouble because they're too afraid to back out, in case they look soft. Peer pressure is very common in gangs.

💀 Although you may not be doing anything illegal, if you're part of a gang, you're more likely to attract the attention of the police. Young people's characters are often judged by who they mix with; if you hang around with a wild lot, outsiders will assume you're the same.

💀 If you are being picked on by a gang, tell your parents, teacher or any other adult in authority. It's difficult to stand up to bullies when they are part of a group and you're on your own – that's why you need adult help. Don't be afraid to ask for it. Call the Anti-Bullying Campaign on 020 7378 1446.

From *Shout*, issue 105 © D.C. Thomson & Co. Ltd

The influence of advertising

Everywhere you go there are advertisements. Advertisers know that the more visible their product is, the more likely you are to buy it. So they are willing to spend large sums of money to promote their goods or services. An advert which interrupts the programme you are watching at peak time on TV may last for less than a minute, but the advertiser is willing to pay the TV company hundreds of thousands of pounds to broadcast it.

The money which advertisers pay to media institutions, such as TV companies, newspapers and magazines, provides them with most of their revenue. Without the money from advertising, the programmes broadcast by independent radio stations and commercial TV companies would not get made, and most of the magazines and newspapers you read would not get published.

Is advertising good or bad?

Some people would argue that it is wrong to use advertising to persuade people to buy things, especially things they might not really need. They also think that many advertisements are not strictly truthful when they claim that this washing powder is new and improved, or that cats love this particular brand of cat food.

The other side of the argument is that without advertising people would be less aware of what was available for them to buy. Also, that if manufacturers compete with one another to produce goods then they must compete to sell them as well.

From *Third Stages*

⊕ In groups

How much do you think you are influenced by advertisements? Talk about your favourite TV ads and why you like them. Are they for products that you are likely to go out and buy? If so, do you think the adverts have made you more likely to go out and buy them?

Discuss the views below. Say why you think advertising is either a good thing or a bad thing.

❝ Advertising encourages people to be materialistic and to want things they don't really need. ❞

❝ There's nothing wrong with advertising. It keeps people informed and encourages competition which benefits everybody. ❞

Some people argue that adverts have less influence than is often made out. They say that most people are suspicious of the claims that advertisers make. They suggest that the most popular TV ads are enjoyed because they are entertaining and funny, rather than because they are informative about the product, and that they don't really influence people to buy the product.

However, there is plenty of evidence to suggest that advertising does work. Retailers are often informed before a TV advertising campaign is about to take place in their area, so that they can stock up on the product in advance, and be in a position to meet the demand for the product that a campaign is likely to generate. Successful campaigns do lead to increased sales.

How much influence do adverts have on you?

the power of advertising

Advertising and children

Advertisements that appear on television are regulated by the Independent Television Commission (ITC). Those that appear on radio are regulated by the Radio Authority. These organisations are independent of the government, the broadcasters and the advertisers. They make sure that all advertisements that are broadcast on the television and radio in the UK are legal, decent, honest and truthful.

The advertising codes drawn up by the ITC and the Radio Authority set out a series of general rules. These rules cover misleading advertisements, price comparisons, taste and decency, discrimination and many other matters. If advertisements fail to follow these rules, they can be altered or banned outright.

The codes contain special rules for advertisers who target children (who are defined as those aged 15 and below). The advertisements 'must not include any material which might result in harm to them either physically, mentally or morally'. The detailed rules that radio advertisers must observe when they target young people are shown above.

Advertising and Children

Rule 1 Misleadingness
Advertisements addressed to the child listener must not exaggerate or mislead about the size, qualities or capabilities of products or about the sounds they might produce.

Rule 2 Prices
Prices of products advertised to children must not be minimised by words such as 'only' or 'just'.

Rule 3 Immaturity and Credulity
Advertisements must not take advantage of the immaturity or natural credulity of children.

Rule 4 Appeals to Loyalty
Advertisements must not take advantage of the sense of loyalty of children or suggest that unless children buy or encourage others to buy a product or service they will be failing in some duty or lacking in loyalty.

Rule 5 Inferiority
Advertisements must not lead children to believe that unless they have or use the product advertised they will be inferior in some way to other children or liable to be held in contempt or ridicule.

Rule 6 Direct Exhortation
Advertisements must not directly urge children to buy products or to ask adults to buy products for them. For example, children must not be directly invited to 'ask Mum' or 'ask Dad' to buy them an advertiser's product.

Rule 7 Direct Response
Advertisements must not invite children to purchase products by mail or telephone.

Rule 8 Competitions
(a) References to competitions for children are acceptable provided that any skill required is appropriate to the age of likely participants and the values of the prizes and the chances of winning are not exaggerated.
(b) The published rules must be submitted in advance to the licensee and the principal conditions of the competition must be included in the advertisement.

Rule 9 Free Gifts
References to 'free' gifts for children in advertisements must include all qualifying conditions, e.g. any time limit, how many products need to be bought, how many wrappers need to be collected, etc.

Rule 10 Health and Hygiene
(a) Advertisements must not encourage children to eat frequently throughout the day.
(b) Advertisements must not encourage children to consume food or drink near bedtime.
(c) Advertisements for confectionery and snack foods must not suggest that such products may be substituted for balanced meals.

Rule 11 Children as Presenters
(a) The participation of children in radio commercials is acceptable, subject to all relevant legal requirements.
(b) If children are employed in commercials, they must not be used to present products or services which they could not be expected to buy themselves. They must not make significant comments on characteristics of products and services about which they could not be expected to have direct knowledge.

Rule 12 Testimonials
Children must not personally testify about products and services. They may, however, give spontaneous comments on matters in which they would have an obvious natural interest.

Radio Authority, Advertising and Sponsorship Code, 1997

In groups

Study carefully the Radio Authority guidelines for advertising and children and discuss the reasons for each part of the code.

In Sweden, television advertisements aimed at children under twelve are banned, because it is argued that young children cannot tell the difference between television advertising and other programmes until they are ten. Sweden would like to see TV adverts aimed at children banned in all EU countries. Do you think such a ban should be introduced in the UK? Give reasons for your views.

Getting the message across

THE COMMERCIAL BREAK

Television advertisers use various techniques to get their message across on television. They mix people and places, words and music with pictures and they choose very carefully what and who they show in their advertisements. The timing of television commercials is very important as well. Advertisers know, from market research, exactly when most mothers, children or families are likely to be viewing. They plan their advertising campaigns accordingly.

People and Places

The people you see in television advertisements are often not like real people. Sometimes they represent a kind of person – a stereotype – and we understand the message the stereotype conveys. For example: if we see a man in a suit carrying a briefcase we recognize a businessman and understand the message is about efficiency; if we see a woman with a baby, feeding or playing with it, we understand the message is about caring. These messages are very important in advertising.

The people in television advertisements are usually attractive, young, quite well-off and white. There are sometimes old people and children, but only if the product is something especially for them. People who are poor, unattractive or physically disabled are hardly ever seen in advertisements.

Sometimes famous people, sports personalities or television stars are paid to advertise products. The advertiser thinks that if you like the person you will believe what they say and trust them. Or you might secretly admire them and want to be like them, so you would like to use the product they advertise.

Words and Music

The words of advertisements are obviously very important. Short, snappy, easy-to-remember slogans are often the key to success in an advertising campaign.

Jingles are those catchy little rhymes and verses which are easy to pick up, sing along with or remember after only one or two hearings.

It is also fashionable now for advertisers to use 'real' music in their advertisements so that the song and the product become closely linked together. If you liked the song that will encourage you to buy the product.

From *Third Stages*

⊕ In groups

Discuss what you learn from the article 'The commercial break' and draw up a list of the various techniques that are used in TV advertisements. Talk about recent TV ads and discuss which of these techniques they use.

Imagine you were in charge of planning a TV advertising campaign for a new product aimed at young people of your age, for example, a new bicycle model. Discuss your ideas for a 30 second advert and prepare a proposal to present to the rest of the class.

Plan and produce a radio advert for a new product. Discuss how many radio adverts include a catchy piece of music with simple lyrics called a jingle. Draft your script, choose appropriate music and compose a jingle to advertise your product. Then make a tape recording of your advert and play it to the rest of the class.

for your file

Find an advert in a newspaper or magazine and write an analysis of it. Comment on what its message is, who it is aimed at and how the words and picture(s) are used to create an image of the product that will encourage the target audience to want to buy it.

Sponsorship

Another way companies use the power of the media to get their message across is through **sponsorship**. One form of sponsorship involves paying for the right to have their name associated with a particular event. An example of this is when a company sponsors a sporting event so that the advertiser's name forms part of the event's title. Football clubs play each other in the FA Carling Premiership or the Nationwide Football League and teams from the lower divisions compete in the Auto Windscreens Shield. Every time the event is reported in the press, on the radio or TV, the sponsor gets a mention.

Another form of sponsorship involves paying teams or individuals to wear names and logos printed on their clothes. In 1999, the sports clothing and shoes manufacturer Nike signed a sponsorship deal with the world's number one golfer, Tiger Woods, worth $90 million over five years. For $18 million a year Woods will wear Nike 'ticks' on the heels and uppers of both shoes, on the back and front of his shirt, on both sleeves, on both collars and on his visor.

When I was 13, my bed was covered in a Take That duvet, my tea was served in a Take That mug and my T-shirt was covered in Take That signs. Now that I'm 19, I'd like to think that I no longer suffer from celebrity endorsed product syndrome. But the other day, I found myself buying some L'Oreal shampoo because I reckoned it was worth it if I ended up with hair like Jennifer Aniston's.

Teens are not duped by the face of a pop star on a can of fizzy drink (do the ad men think we believe drinking Coke is going to give us the voice of a Number One singer?). But sometimes, the power of a star can get us to buy the product. It just has to be done the right way.

For a start, the celebrity and the item have to go together. According to a survey, a massive 77 per cent of people remember that Bob Hoskins did the BT ads, but I very much doubt that the figure would be matched if he was advertising Brylcreem à la David Beckham. And the beautiful face of Madonna works well with Max Factor, but you wouldn't pop down to the chemist to buy a lippie if she was replaced by Mrs Merton.

Celebrity endorsement

Would you buy something just because a famous person plugged it? 'It depends,' says Bryony Gordon, 19, 'on the star and the product.'

The products celebrities push and why

MADONNA: Max Factor 'She was chosen as she's so glamorous,' say the cosmetic giants.

MICHAEL OWEN: Walkers Crisps 'Michael is the perfect combination of the England schoolboy system and, of course, a national celebrity,' Walkers said.

KATE MOSS: L'Oreal Picked because 'Kate represents youth and glamour – and she's got great, silky hair.'

blond californien

From *The Daily Telegraph*, 28 August 1999

In groups

Discuss what Bryony Gordon says about the use of celebrities to endorse products. Do you agree with her views? Explain why.

Are you making the most of your leisure time?

Do this quiz to find out about how well you spend your leisure time. Keep a record of your answers, and then check what your answers tell you about what use you make of your leisure time.

A test-yourself quiz

1 **At the weekend do you:**
a *always plan in advance what you are going to do;*
b *sometimes plan things in advance;*
c *never plan ahead – just wait to see what happens?*

2 **How much time do you spend each week on your hobby?**
a *4–6 hours;*
b *1–3 hours;*
c *less than an hour a week.*

3 **What types of TV programmes do you mainly watch?**
a *'serious' programmes, such as documentaries, news and drama;*
b *a mixture of serious programmes and light entertainment;*
c *light entertainment, such as comedies, soaps, pop music and quizzes.*

4 **How often do you stay after school for a club or a practice?**
a *2 or 3 times a week;* **b** *once a week;*
c *hardly ever.*

5 **When you go out with your friends do you usually:**
a *go somewhere to do something, for example, go to a film or a disco, or to a park to play football;*
b *go shopping or to a café;*
c *hang about hoping someone might suggest something to do?*

6 **How often do you read a book other than a schoolbook?**
a *most days;*
b *every now and then;*
c *hardly ever.*

7 **How often do you take exercise (apart from in PE lessons)?**
a *5–6 days a week;*
b *2–3 days a week;*
c *hardly ever.*

8 **When you go on a computer what do you mostly use it for?**
a *finding information from the Internet;*
b *sending e-mails to friends and relatives;*
c *playing games.*

making the most of your leisure

 How do you keep up with what's going on in the world?

a by watching the news/reading a newspaper daily;
b by watching the news every now and then;
c by relying on other people to tell you if something happens.

 If you are asked to volunteer to take part in a community activity do you usually:

a volunteer;
b wait to see if your friends do, then volunteer;
c never volunteer?

 How often in the holidays do you feel bored because you can't think of anything to do?

a very rarely;   **b** sometimes;   **c** most days.

 How much time each day do you spend watching TV?

a less than 1 hour;
b between 1 and 3 hours;
c over 3 hours.

What your answers say about how you spend your leisure time

Mostly 'a's You make very good use of your leisure time. You have plenty of interests and hobbies and you plan activities to do at the weekend and with your friends. You are prepared to volunteer for things and are involved in after-school activities. You look after yourself too by taking plenty of exercise. So you shouldn't get bored. But make sure you don't wear yourself out with all your activities. Allow yourself some time just to relax!

Mostly 'b's *Your attitude to your leisure time is the same as many people's. Sometimes you plan ahead and you get actively involved in the things you like doing on a fairly regular basis. You've got a more relaxed attitude to life than the people who get mostly 'a's. But you could be making better use of your leisure time than you are. If you want to achieve more in your leisure pursuits, you'll need to put your mind to doing so.*

Mostly 'c's You're not getting as much out of your leisure time as you could be. If your life seems boring much of the time, then you need to ask yourself why. Things won't change unless you do something to make them. Otherwise you'll continue to drift through life getting less out of it than you could be.

In pairs

Talk about what you have learned from this activity. How well do you use your leisure time and how good are you at:

- planning how you spend your time;
- getting involved in activities at school and in the community;
- using your leisure time to develop your knowledge and skills?

Each decide on one or more things you could do to make better use of your leisure time.

Four Ways to Make Better Use of Your Leisure Time

1 **Ration how much TV you watch.**
2 **Stay at school once a week for an after-school club.**
3 **Go out for a jog or a bike ride every other day.**
4 **Spend at least 20 minutes a day reading a book, magazine or newspaper.**

I never have any time to myself

" *My problem is I hardly get any time to myself. By the time I've done my chores and then my homework, I'm exhausted. All I want to do is watch TV or listen to my CDs. And at the weekend I never have any time to myself because I'm expected to do things with the family. What can I do? It's really getting me down.* " – Peta

for your file

Read Peta's letter (left). Write a reply to Peta advising her on how to deal with her problem.

Beating the boredom blues

So it's the school holidays. For once you've got time on your hands. The trouble is: you don't seem to know what to do with it. Samantha Graham suggests ten things you can do to beat those school holiday boredom blues.

Getting a Piece of the Action

1. Join The Club
Many youth clubs run schemes for teenagers during the holidays, or there may be one being run at your school. Go and find out what's on offer by asking at your local community centre or looking in the community newsletter.

2. Go Exploring
Investigate the area where you live. Many people never bother to visit the interesting places in their neighbourhood. Find out about places you can visit and things to see in your area from the local tourist information office or from your local library.

3. Get Into Shape
Oh no! I hear you groan, but getting fit can be fun. One of the best forms of exercise is swimming, another is cycling. You don't need to have a 21-gear racer or a mountain bike. You can go at your own speed and explore all those places that you've never got round to seeing.

4. Go Green
Contact organisations like Friends of the Earth and see if there are any local schemes to protect the environment that you can get involved in. Or organise your own scheme. For example, get together with some friends and set up a recycling team.

5. Do-It-Yourself
Do a deal with your parents. Say that if they let you redesign and redecorate your bedroom and supply you with the materials, you'll do the work yourself. You'll not only learn all about painting and decorating, but you'll also end up with the bedroom you've always wanted.

6. Put It In Writing
Get your pen and paper out and get writing. So you never got round to keeping a diary? Well, now's the time to start! Or what about that story that's been lurking at the back of your mind, or that letter you said you'd write to the newspaper in protest about cruelty to animals? Get scribbling.

7. Get Crafty
Ask your mum or dad if you can borrow their tools and get out into the shed and make something for yourself. What about a new CD rack? Raid your money box to buy some of that material you fancied and make yourself something new to wear. Use your practical skills – get crafty!

8. Get In On The Act
Join the local drama club and get involved in their productions. You don't fancy acting? Then get a back-stage role, looking after the lighting, painting the scenery, making the costumes or doing the make-up. Or get together with your friends, borrow a video camera and make your own video.

9. Read All About It
Get down to the local library and borrow those expensive books about your hobby that you couldn't afford to buy. Become more of an expert than you already are on the things that really interest you.

10. Get Connected
Everyone's been telling you to develop your computer skills. Well, now's your chance. Get on-line and search the net for websites about your favourite subject. Find an e-mail buddy who's into your hobby and swap information and advice. You could even design your own newsletter to send to your family and friends.

⊕ In groups

Discuss Samantha Graham's suggestions. Talk about the ones which appeal to you most and the ones which appeal to you least. Can you suggest other ways of beating boredom and making the most of your leisure time? Keep notes of your ideas and share them in a class discussion.

Choose your exercise

One way you can use your leisure time well is to make sure you get enough exercise. The fitter you are, the more energy you will have. The more energy you have, the more you will be able to get out of life.

True physical fitness is something more than simply being fit to cope with the stresses and strains of everyday life. It consists of three important ingredients – stamina, suppleness and strength – the S-factors (see box).

First and most important is **STAMINA**. This is staying power, endurance, the ability to keep going without gasping for breath. For stamina, you need a well-developed circulation in the heart and lungs so that plenty of vital oxygen is pumped to your working muscles. With stamina you have a slower, more powerful heartbeat. You can cope more easily with prolonged or heavy exertion.

Next is **SUPPLENESS** or flexibility. You need to develop maximum range of movement of your neck, spine and joints to avoid spraining ligaments and pulling muscles and tendons. The more mobile you are, the less likely you'll suffer aches and pains brought on by stiffness.

Finally, **STRENGTH**. Extra muscle-power in reserve for those often unexpected heavier jobs. Lifting and shifting need strong shoulder, trunk and thigh muscles. Toned-up tummy muscles help to take the strain … and keep your waistline trim.

From *Print-Base* 1, by
John Foster

for your file

" Why do adults make such a fuss about teenagers taking exercise? I can't see the point myself. As far as I'm concerned exercise is a waste of time. " – Sam

Write a reply to Sam explaining why exercise is important and suggesting the different ways she or he could get some exercise.

S-FACTOR SCORE

	Stamina	Suppleness	Strength
Badminton	**	***	**
Canoeing	***	**	***
Climbing Stairs	***	*	**
Cricket	*	**	*
Cycling (hard)	****	**	***
Dancing (ballroom)	*	***	*
Dancing (disco)	***	****	*
Digging (garden)	***	**	****
Football	***	***	***
Golf	*	**	*
Gymnastics	**	****	***
Hill Walking	***	*	**
Housework (moderate)	*	**	*
Jogging	****	**	**
Judo	**	****	**
Mowing lawn by hand	**	**	***
Rowing	****	**	****
Sailing	*	**	**
Squash	***	***	**
Swimming (hard)	****	****	****
Tennis	**	***	**
Walking (briskly)	**	*	*
Weightlifting	*	*	****
Yoga	*	****	*

* No real effect   *** Very good effect
** Beneficial effect   **** Excellent effect

In pairs

Talk about the S-factors, discussing why each one is important.

Study the S-factor score chart. Work out a test-yourself quiz, consisting of statements some of which are true and some of which are false, then give the quiz to another group to do. Here is one possible question:

1. Housework builds up your stamina more than digging. True or false?

Alcohol – the facts

What's all the fuss about?

People have made and drunk alcohol for thousands of years, and alcohol is certainly part of everyday life in our society. You may drink to be sociable, to relax or because you like it, and there doesn't seem any harm in that. But alcohol is a powerful and potentially addictive drug, and you need to be aware of its effects, especially if you misuse it.

In the short term

When you drink, the alcohol is absorbed into your bloodstream. It takes about five to ten minutes to take effect, but the effects can last for several hours. Of course, how alcohol affects you depends on how much you have drunk, how quickly you've drunk it, how strong it is (spirits are stronger than beer, for example) and whether you've had anything to eat beforehand (a good move, if you don't want to risk a hangover).

And the effects? Well, as you probably know, alcohol can make you feel great – relaxed, confident etc. It can also make you feel terrible: sick, dizzy, headachy, clumsy. It's a bit of a myth that alcohol cheers people up – it is actually a depressant and you may end up crying into your drink rather than having a laugh.

Because alcohol reduces self control, there's a real danger of people hurting themselves or others (by accident or on purpose!). There's the risk of drinking too much, falling asleep and choking on their own vomit. Then there's the hangover – waking up and knowing that if you move your head will split open, but you have to get up and go to school or work.

Never mix alcohol with other drugs – it can be fatal.

In the long term

If you're healthy anyway, and if you drink in moderation (i.e. at most a couple of drinks a day), you shouldn't have a long-term problem with alcohol. But if you drink heavily over a long period you run the risk of brain damage, liver disease (called cirrhosis), mouth and throat cancer, heart problems and stomach ulcers. Most of these can be fatal.

People often forget that alcohol is full of calories, hence the 'beer gut' of heavy beer drinkers. One pint of beer contains about 180 calories.

Alcohol can be addictive and you can become dependent on it. Several hundred thousand people in Britain are thought to be alcoholics. Some of them are not much older than you.

Drink strengths

People often think that certain drinks, such as beer or cider, contain less alcohol than others. In fact, a half pint of ordinary strength beer or cider has about the same amount of alcohol in it as a normal glass of wine or a pub measure of whisky.

1 unit =

| half a pint of ordinary beer or cider | a single measure of spirits (whisky, gin, bacardi, vodka, etc.) | a standard glass of wine | a small glass of sherry |

The alcohol content of drinks is measured in units. The safe limits for adults are considered to be 14 units a week for women and 21 units a week for men. Depending on your age and your size, your safe limits may be much lower.

On average it takes an hour for the alcohol to register in the body, and then one hour per unit of alcohol drunk for it to disappear.

Did you know?

It is dangerous to drink when you are pregnant. Heavy drinking can affect the baby's health and weight at birth.

⊕ In groups

❝ *People who don't drink are party-poopers. They just don't know how to have a good time. Why should we take any notice of what they say? The risks of drinking are exaggerated.* ❞ Kirstie (15)

❝ *I think the people of my age who drink are immature. They do it to show off and try to make themselves popular. But they don't impress me when they start throwing up.* ❞ Shareen (14)

Discuss the views of these young people and say why you agree or disagree with them.

Adapted from *Drugs*, by Anita Ganeri

drinking and alcohol

Alcohol and Young People – the Law

Buying alcohol You are not allowed to buy alcohol until you are 18. A shopkeeper or pub landlord can be prosecuted for selling alcohol to anyone under 18. If you are under 18 and try to buy or drink alcohol on licensed premises you can be fined. Anyone who buys you a drink in a bar when you are under 18 is committing an offence. But over 16 year olds can be bought some drinks in a restaurant to have with a meal – beer and cider in England and Wales; beer, cider and wine in Scotland.

Drinking alcohol When you are 14 you are allowed to go into a licensed bar, but it is an offence for you to drink alcohol in a licensed bar if you are under 18. The police can confiscate alcohol from anyone under 18 who is drinking it in a public place. However, it is not illegal for under 18s to drink alcohol either at home or at someone else's home.

PLANNING TO GET REALLY DRUNK?

Every year 1000 young people under 15 are admitted to hospital suffering from acute alcohol poisoning. Not everyone makes it. It doesn't always stop at being sick.

But drinking's all about being sociable. Everyone knows that. Well, that depends on how much and why you drink. If you don't go over the top then, sure, you can be more lively and friendly. But haven't you noticed how people who really have had too much aren't worth talking to? They either make total idiots of themselves or end up getting ignored.

GETTING DRUNK

AND HOW ABOUT LOOKING GOOD?

All the people we spoke to said they never fancied drunks. Think about it. Would you like to kiss a drunk?

And what about those stupid things we do when we've had a few too many? Some you can laugh about the day after – some you can't.

You're probably aware of all the people killed and injured on bikes and in cars because of drink. But have you thought of all the other problems of drinking too much?

Drinking is attractive

It's easy to get into a fight, to have a row with a friend, even to get charged by the police. That's happening more and more. What begins as a laugh ends up as more than a joke.

And what about sex? Anyone can make mistakes about sex when drunk. This can lead to unwanted pregnancies and the risk of catching sexually transmitted diseases.

From A D.I.Y. Guide to Sensible Drinking for Young People

In groups

What does the article 'Getting drunk' suggest are the risks a person runs if they get very drunk? What do you think of people who get very drunk? How would you describe their behaviour – funny? stupid? disgusting? immature?

What is your opinion of someone who deliberately tries to get someone else drunk?

In pairs

Study the information on these two pages and produce a True or False quiz, consisting of statements about alcohol and drinking. Then give the quiz to another pair to do.

for your file

Design a poster called 'Think Before You Drink' to make young people of your age aware of how drinking can affect them.

Problem drinking

Andrew's Story

'I was like most other 16 year olds. We drank and enjoyed getting drunk regularly. It was great. I loved the buzz and never thought there were any problems. I always drank more than my mates – always.'

He left school rather than stay on to study and apply for university and took a job in the catering trade. 'The first people I fell in with at work drank and soon I was always drunk. Strangers would want to fight me because of something I had said or done the night before, but I never considered myself addicted.'

To add to his earlier pattern of heavy drinking, he now drank to get through the day and could no longer stop at will. 'I still saw no reason to stop.'

Perched at the top of the slippery slope of dependence, he plunged rapidly to the bottom. His girlfriend left him and he was sacked. Andrew's dad told him to get himself sorted and find a new job and gave him some money. 'But I drank away the money and, within three weeks, ended up in a hostel for the homeless. I would steal, sell things and do anything to get alcohol, though I stopped short of violence. Then the hallucinations started. I was convinced that an army of down-and-outs wanted to find me and kill me.'

He was terrified, and for the first time realised that he must get help to stop drinking. He was admitted to a psychiatric hospital. 'I was there for four weeks. You are in meetings with others who have been through it all, and I could be completely honest. The best thing is that the hospital rebuilt my confidence.'

Fortunately, his family were completely supportive. Andrew has now got a job as a computer programmer and been sober for 18 months. He accepts he must never drink alcohol again. 'I keep up with my friends from the hospital and go to AA meetings if I feel down. But I can drink a Coke in a pub quite happily.'

To teenage drinkers he says: 'Beware if you begin to feel you don't like being sober. There is no point in my looking back now; I have to accept that I became an alcoholic.'

>>> KERRY'S STORY >>>

Kerry, 14, started drinking for a laugh with her mates. But now she's relying on it more and more ...

'If you'd said to me a while ago that I'd be drinking most weekends when I reached this age, I'd never have believed you. When I was younger and my mum and dad let me try their drinks, I always thought they were disgusting – I couldn't see why anyone would want to drink them because they tasted so horrible.

CONFIDENCE

'That all changed when my mate Ailsa got her brother to buy us some cider one night. We were supposed to be seeing some lads in the park later on and we had it before we met them. Ailsa said it tasted okay and would give us confidence and she was right – I couldn't believe how good it made me feel. I've always been quite a shy and nervous person, but after a few swigs of cider, I felt really good. Ailsa and I were laughing at everything and I became much more loud and confident. I felt really good about myself – much better than I normally did.

'That night we met the lads in the park. Normally, I'd have been so quiet and shy with them, but because I'd had some cider I felt great and I actually got off with James, the boy I'd fancied for ages.

CIDER

'After that Ailsa and I would split a bottle of cider between us whenever we were going somewhere, like to a mate's party. Then I started feeling like I needed a drink to get me in the mood for enjoying myself, even if we were just going down the park to hang around. If I haven't had a drink and there are lads there I feel all panicky and shaky and don't usually say much to them.

'I spend a fortune on breath fresheners because my mum would kill me if she ever found out that I'm drinking, and all my pocket money seems to go on cider these days. I know I'm probably relying on drink too much now but at least I'm having fun.'

Valerie's Story

'My father died when I was nine and I think it was then that my mother started drinking heavily. It was a horrific situation because I felt so helpless. I would come home and she'd be sitting in front of the TV completely drunk. Very often there would be no food on the table and no money to buy any because she'd spent it all on drink. Sometimes I'd have to go round to a friend's house and beg them to lend us some money – it was so humiliating.'

Gradually her mother's problem became more serious and it was Valerie who had to run the home. 'I had two younger brothers to look after as well, which was no joke. I used to come home with heaps of homework only to spend my evenings cooking, cleaning and doing the laundry. It was very difficult because I really wanted to go to university but I couldn't fit in time for studying.'

For Valerie, the worst thing was the uncertainty. 'I'd never know quite what to expect when I came home. One day I'd come in and she'd be rolling around on the kitchen floor, so drunk that she'd wet herself. I would have to clean her up and put her to bed like a baby.'

Valerie tried everything she could. She joined a local branch of Alateen. She tried to get her mother to join a support group to kick the habit. But although her mother tried to change, the attempts were usually short-lived. 'I felt very guilty about it. I began to think that maybe I was to blame for her drinking, and that I had to make her stop. I also felt guilty about wanting to leave and go to college when I knew that there would be no one to look after her or my younger brothers, and I realised that I had to make a difficult choice.'

In the end she got a place at a college 20 miles away so she could still live at home. Now 20 and in her second year, she is finding it more and more difficult to keep up with course work and look after the family. 'I'm a bit fed up because I am missing out on all the social life and, whenever a guy asks me out, I usually have to turn him down. I sometimes wish that someone would pay attention to me for a change – Mum has always been the centre of attention because of her problem. All I can hope is that one day she will get over this.'

Adapted from 'Stolen Childhood', by Anita Chaudhuri in *19*, 19 October 1991

In groups

Discuss Andrew's story. What do you learn about how to spot a drinking problem, and how to deal with it?

Discuss Kerry's story. Is she just 'having fun'?

Discuss the problems that Valerie has had to face because of her mother's alcoholism. What do you learn about what it feels like to have a parent with a drinking problem?

for your file

Study the advice on how to cope. Imagine you write an advice column for a teenage magazine. Write your reply to a letter from Tony (13) who lives alone with his father. His father has a drink problem and Tony is trying to cope.

Living with Someone who Drinks – How to Cope

- Look after yourself and take steps to protect yourself, especially if you think you might be at risk.
- Don't blame yourself for their drinking. Each adult is responsible for him or herself.
- Don't pour away alcohol unless someone asks you. Taking alcohol from someone who is already drunk may put you at risk of being hurt.
- Don't cover up or make excuses to other people for their drinking.
- Don't be afraid to voice your concerns when they are sober.
- Tell another adult you trust what's going on. Share the burden.
- Contact Alateen and Al-Anon Family Groups. They are organisations which aim to help families of problem drinkers. Alateen deal specifically with teenagers who have been, or still are, affected by an alcoholic relative. The organisation is completely confidential.

ALATEEN, 61 Great Dover Street, London SE1 4YF
Tel: 020 7403 0888
AL-ANON FAMILY GROUPS, 61 Great Dover Street, London SE1 4YF

From *Wise Guides: Drugs*, by Anita Naik

13 You and the community –

Change and the school community – the five-term year

Your school is a community of people with a common aim – to provide you with an education that will enable you to make the fullest use of your talents and that will prepare you for life as an adult citizen.

The school community is made up of lots of different groups of people: students, teachers, classroom assistants, administrative staff, caretaking and cleaning staff, parents and governors. Whenever a major change is made – for example, to the size of the school, the hours of the school day or the number of terms in the school year – it will affect all these groups.

A new school year?

In January 2000 a government inquiry was set up to look at the advantages and disadvantages of changing the school year to either four or five terms.

The Four-Term Year
1. September–October, then a 2-week break
2. November–December, then a 2-week break
3. January–Easter, then a 2-week break
4. Easter–July, with a 1-week half-term break, then a 5-week summer holiday

The Five-Term Year
1. September–October, then a 2-week break
2. November–December, then a Christmas break
3. January–March, then a 2-week break
4. April–May, then a 2-week break
5. June–July, then a 4-week summer holiday

School Calendar Shake-Up

Schools could switch from three terms a year to five – with one set aside for pupils to have fun.

The change would allow more time for schoolchildren to enjoy arts, sport and creative activities, according to the head of an inquiry into reforming the school year.

Christopher Price, former Labour MP and university chancellor, is to lead a six-month investigation for the Local Government Association, with many local education authorities keen to move to a five-term year.

The most likely formula is five eight-week terms separated by four two-week breaks and a summer holiday cut from six weeks to four. Total holidays would remain the same.

Many councils believe this could ease pressure on teachers by spreading their workload more evenly. It could also stop children forgetting much of what they have learned during the long summer break.

Schools could also devote the summer term to creativity. Critics of the Government's drive to improve classroom standards have complained that arts, sport and creative activities are being squeezed out by 'discipline and rote'.

Many parents had great difficulty keeping their children occupied during the long summer holiday or arranging for their youngsters to be cared for while they went to work. In addition, the cost of family holidays was highest at that time.

There was also evidence that many pupils slipped backwards in learning during the summer holidays.

The review will examine all possibilities for change, including bringing forward the exam season. Moving exams from May and June to April and May could ease the present scramble for university places and free a new summer term for broader activities.

Adapted from an article by T...

the school as a community

A change for the better?

Here are some reactions to the proposal to change to a five-term year.

> ❝ *How would everyone manage to fit in their holidays during only a four-week summer break? It's hard enough as it is trying to get time off when everyone else wants it.* ❞
> – Parent

> ❝ *It would increase the pressure on teachers, who would lose the advantage of having a long block of time in the summer in which to do detailed planning.* ❞ – Teacher

> ❝ *It might ease the frantic scramble there is at the beginning of the autumn term to sort everything out, by spreading things over the year a bit more.* ❞ – School secretary

> ❝ *You don't want to be in school in the summer when it's hot, even if you're supposedly having fun. I'd much rather have a long summer holiday than lots of short breaks throughout the year.* ❞ – Student

> ❝ *I'm all for it. Children get out of the habit of studying during the summer holiday. It's always a fight to get them to do their homework when they go back in the autumn.* ❞
> – Parent

> ❝ *We do a lot of maintenance work in the summer holidays at present. But we should be able to fit it in whatever the pattern of the school year.* ❞ – Caretaker

> ❝ *Research shows that many children have forgotten what they have learned when they return to school after a six-week break. I think it would help us to improve the school's academic results.* ❞ – Governor

⊕ In groups

List what you think to be the advantages and disadvantages of having a five-term school year, taking into consideration how it would affect all members of the school community.

Organise a debate on the motion: 'This house believes that a five-term school year is better than a three-term school year.'

The school day

⊕ In groups

Talk about how your school day is organised. Imagine you have been asked to inquire into ways of changing it. What are the arguments for and against:

a an earlier start or a later start;
b longer or shorter morning/afternoon breaks;
c a longer lunch hour;
d an earlier or a later finishing time?

Consider other ideas, such as reorganising the lesson timetable so that all the lessons take place on four and a half days – activities could then be organised on the other half-day to allow students to pursue their own interests. In your discussions, take into consideration how your suggestions would affect the various different members of the school's community.

Decide whether or not you recommend any changes to the school day. Appoint a spokesperson to report your conclusions to the rest of the class in a class discussion.

You and the community – the school as a community

Participating in the school community

School councils

Most schools have a school council which exists to let the teachers and headteacher know what students' opinions are on a range of school issues. The school council usually consists of two or three elected representatives from each year group.

Year councils

Because school councils are sometimes dominated by older students, some schools have introduced year councils. The aim of a year council is to give students the opportunity to express opinions on matters of importance to that particular year group.

Our school council meets once every three weeks. It discusses issues such as the dress code, the use of social areas, charity fundraising and bullying.

Beach Lane School Year 8 Council – Constitution

1. The council's purpose is to act as a forum for discussion of school issues relevant to Year 8, and to let the teachers and headteacher know what student opinion is on these issues. The council will also take responsibility for co-operating with year staff in the organisation of one social event per term for Year 8.

2. Membership of the council will consist of three representatives from each class, elected on a termly basis.

3. Meetings will be held once a fortnight. The council members will elect a chair to control the meetings and a secretary who will be responsible for circulating the agenda for each meeting and taking and circulating minutes of meetings.

4. The class representatives will be responsible for giving a report of the council's meetings to their class. Agenda and minutes of meetings will be put up in each classroom.

5. The Year 8 council will elect two of its members to be members of the school council, with responsibility for raising issues on behalf of Year 8 students at school council meetings.

6. The chair, secretary and school council representatives will be responsible for taking up matters raised at council meetings with the year head and other teachers, and for reporting back on such matters to the Year 8 council.

7. The head of year will attend all council meetings as an observer and both they and the other year staff will be available as required to offer support and advice to council members and to assist in the settlement of disputes.

In groups

Imagine that elections are about to be held for class representatives to the Year 8 council. Choose one of the group to stand as a candidate. Together draft a statement of the issues you think the Year 8 council should take up for your candidate to present to the rest of the class to explain why she or he should be elected. Then listen to the various candidates' statements and hold a mock election to elect two representatives.

Imagine that the school is currently revising its dress code and the year council is being asked for its views. Study the current Year 8 uniform requirements and suggest how you would like to alter them. Make notes of your views and share your ideas in a class discussion.

for your file

Write a letter to the school council on a Year 8 issue (for example, the lack of a social area for Year 8 students at break times; the need to improve the provision of lockers and locker space for Year 8 students; the amount of bullying of Year 8s by older students), asking the school council to discuss the issue and take it up with the teaching staff.

Organising a social event

This page explains how your class can work together to organise a social event.

There are various types of social event you could organise:

An ice-skating trip

A theatre trip to a play, a concert or show

A visit to the Millennium Dome

A trip to an international sports event

A Year 8 disco

A visit to a theme park

Planning the event

⊕ In groups

Discuss your ideas for a social event. Then share your ideas in a class discussion and hold a vote to decide what type of social event your class would like to organise.

Make a list of all the jobs that will have to be done in order for the event to take place. Then, share your ideas and draw up a complete list of everything that needs to be done (see 8L's list, right).

A planning committee

Once you have decided on the event and listed the jobs to be done, appoint a planning committee. The advantage of having a planning committee is that you can arrange for it to meet regularly to check that everything has been done and to deal with any problems that may arise.

Reviewing the event

After the event, hold a class discussion. Talk about what went well, the problems you faced while organising it, and how you coped with them. What were the strengths and weaknesses of how you organised the event? What lessons did you learn? How would you do things differently, if you were to organise a similar event in the future?

8L Ice-Skating Trip

Checklist of tasks for planning committee

- Choose date and check school calendar to check that it doesn't clash with any other event.
- Contact ice-rink to check opening times, cost of entrance, skate hire and what refreshments are on sale.
- Contact bus company to check availability and cost of coach, and book coach.
- Advertise the trip and get people to sign up for it.
- Check Health and Safety Regulations to ensure that there are enough adults available to come on trip.
- Send out letter to inform parents of arrangements for trip.
- Arrange for collection of money to pay for the coach.

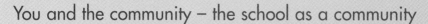

Producing a Year 8 newsletter

These pages explain how your class can work together to plan and publish a Year 8 newsletter.

An editorial committee

In order to co-ordinate the production of the newsletter, you will need an editorial committee.

The role of the editorial committee is:

- to make decisions about the contents and format of the newsletter;
- to draw up a schedule for the production of the newsletter;
- to allocate tasks to individuals and groups;
- to monitor progress and to check that tasks are completed on schedule;
- to design and edit the pages and oversee the printing of the newsletter.

To do this, the editorial committee will need to meet regularly, for example, at the beginning of each session in which you are working on the newsletter.

Working groups

You will also need various working groups. Their role is to carry out the tasks allocated to them by the editorial committee.

Split the class into working groups and then set up an editorial committee by each electing a representative to be on the editorial committee.

Planning the newsletter

When planning what contents to put in your newsletter, you need to think about your target audience and the type of newsletter you are going to produce. Are you planning to produce a newsletter that will be of interest to all the members of the school community or just one specific group, such as students or parents? Is the purpose of your newsletter solely to convey information about the school and school events or is its purpose to entertain as well as to inform?

Once you are clear about the target audience and the purpose of your newsletter, you can draw up a list of suggestions for the contents.

⊕ In groups

Discuss your views on who the target audience should be and what purpose you think the newsletter should have, and draw up a list of proposed contents. Carry out some market research by producing a questionnaire, asking members of your target audience what types of information and articles they would like to see in the newsletter.

Draft a statement of your views for your representative to report to the editorial committee. Then get the editorial committee to hold an open meeting at which the representatives present each group's views. The committee then makes its decisions.

Designing and producing the newsletter

Use a desktop publishing program to design, write, edit and publish the newsletter.

⊞ In groups

Discuss ideas for the format of the newsletter. Which would be better – a two-sided unfolded A4 sheet or a folded leaflet? If you think a leaflet is a good idea, make a mock-up using the actual size of paper and think about how you are going to fold it. Is there a machine available that would fold it, or would it have to be folded by hand?

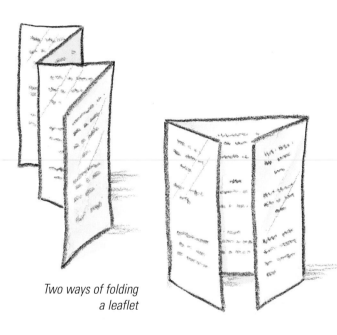

Two ways of folding a leaflet

Think about what kind of layout would be best. Look at different ways of dividing your pages into columns by putting various grids up on the screen.

Look at various typefaces and choose a typeface that would be easy to read.

List the advantages and disadvantages of different formats, layouts and typefaces and get your representative to report your views to the editorial committee. Then hold a meeting of the editorial committee to make a decision on the format of the newsletter.

Drawing up a schedule and producing the contents

Having decided on the format for the newsletter, the editorial committee next needs to decide on a date for the publication of the first issue and to draw up a production schedule.

The committee needs to decide on the contents of the first issue. Once the list of contents has been drawn up, they should appoint page editors. The page editor's job is to fit each article onto the page grid. It is important to have a preliminary plan for the page so that the people who are going to write the articles know approximately how long they should be.

The committee then needs to allocate responsibility for writing each of the articles to different groups. For example, one group could be responsible for articles on studying and book reviews, another group for news items and another for sports reports. The production schedule needs to make clear the deadline by which the articles have to be written.

Editing the pages

Once they have received all the articles, it is the page editor's job to fit them onto the grid. The length of some articles may have to be cut. The headings and sub-headings may have to be changed and rewritten. Illustrations may have to be reduced in size to fit the space available and captions may need to be written.

Printing the newsletter

Once all the pages are edited, run off proof copies of the newsletter and get several members of the class to proofread them, making a final check for any spelling or punctuation errors. Then make any last-minute corrections before printing and distributing your newsletter.

Facts and opinions

Whenever you discuss an issue, it is important to listen to other people's views, to consider their arguments and, if they are convincing, to change your mind about what you think.

In order to be able to judge the strength of other people's arguments, you need to be able to distinguish whether what they are saying is a **fact** or an **opinion**.

A **fact** is a true statement. It can be about an event or thing that is known to have happened or about something which can be shown to be true by experience or observation. For example:

❝ *Many animals which are seriously ill and dying suffer a lot of pain.* ❞

An **opinion** is a judgement or belief. It is a statement of a point of view based on what a person thinks and feels. For example:

❝ *Dying animals should be put down.* ❞

When someone is explaining the reasons why they hold an opinion, they often use a fact to support their view. For example:

❝ *Dying animals should be put down, because many animals which are seriously ill and dying suffer a lot of pain.* ❞

In pairs

Study the list of statements (below) and decide which are facts and which are opinions.

1 Tongue-piercing can cause infections.
2 Body-piercing improves your looks.
3 Animals should be left to die completely natural deaths.
4 Vets can advise you whether or not your pet is terminally ill.
5 There are a number of decisions which 12-year-olds cannot make for themselves.
6 Twelve-year-old children are good at making decisions.
7 There is too much violence in television programmes.

Forming your opinion

Before you take part in any discussion ...

◆ Find out the facts. For example, by reading articles on the subject or looking for information in the library and on the Internet. Check that any information you already have is correct and up to date.

◆ Identify what the main issue is and what different opinions people have. Note down the arguments that are used for and against a particular point of view and any facts and examples used to support those arguments.

◆ Decide what your opinion is. Make a list of arguments why you hold that opinion.

During the discussion ...

◆ Listen to what other people have to say. Note down any new arguments that people introduce or any key facts which you learn from them.

◆ If you find other people's opinions convincing, be prepared to alter your own opinion. However, if you think you are right, don't be pressurised into changing your opinion just because other people don't agree with you. Each of you has a right to their own opinion and you should agree to differ.

8 Some popular cartoon series contain scenes of violence.
9 Many roads get congested around the time that schools start.
10 Pupils who live within three miles of their school should always walk or cycle to school.

Body-piercing – what's your verdict?

Should body-piercing be banned?

NO says Kit, 16

'I can't believe everyone makes such a big deal about body-piercing when it's not hurting anyone except the person who gets it done.

It looks good and original. The trouble is parents completely freak when you say you want one because they think of people with piercings all over their body. I would never do that. All I want is a single stud over my eye which is totally different.

It annoys me that people with piercings get a bad reputation, too. People think that you're a thug. That's stupid. Quite a few of my friends have had their belly pierced or a stud put in their tongue. It doesn't make them bad people; it doesn't change their personality.

Safety is something I think about. But unless you're stupid enough to do one yourself, the risks are low. All the proper shops are hygienic so you're more likely to get knocked down by a bus than get an infection.'

YES says Kit's mother, Candy

'I know that piercing is fashionable but it looks so ugly and primitive. I don't want people to judge Kit badly because he's got a piece of metal sticking out of his face.

If Kit has an eyebrow pierced he'll have to look at it every day of his life – and I'm worried that he'll regret that later on. It's all very well saying that it's not forever. Even if he took it out he could be left with a bad scar.

I don't even want to think about the health risks. Kit tells me piercing shops sterilise their equipment, but there are no guarantees. I'm not stupid. I know there are still a lot of places that are really unhygienic. It's easy to get an infection from a dirty piercing gun.'

Sickening sight!

I think the whole idea of body-piercing is quite sick! Who would want to walk down the street with their nose, eyebrow and other body parts pierced?

Ear-piercing is fine but some people go way over the top by piercing other parts of their body. Several girls in my school think that having a pierced belly button is cool. No chance!

Andrew Thompson in *T2*, 12 June 1999

❝ *There is no official age limit under which you are not allowed to do body-piercing, but we suggest members use their own ethics and morals. We would support some sort of legislation or guidelines.* ❞
– Zoe Rockliffe, secretary of the European Professional Piercing Association

◯ On your own

Study the information and views about body-piercing given in the articles on this page. Make notes on the facts and opinions they contain. Form your own opinion about body-piercing and identify the arguments you are going to use to support your opinion.

✚ In groups

Discuss your views on body-piercing.

for your file

Write a short statement expressing your opinion on body-piercing, explaining why you have or have not changed your mind as a result of the discussion.

Dentists warn of piercing perils

Tongue-piercing can cause infections, interfere with breathing, damage the teeth and lead to speech impediments, say dentists.

'People having tongue-piercings are putting not just their oral health, but their general health at risk – and we strongly advise people not to,' said Dr Geoff Craig of the British Dental Association. 'If people insist on having piercings, they should ensure

that the equipment is sterilised properly and that the stud is made of gold, surgical steel or titanium.'

Adapted from a report in *The Daily Telegraph*, 21 July 1999

You and your opinions – speaking your mind

Debating the issue

A debate is a formal discussion in which two opposing arguments are put forward.

The rules of debating

The meeting is opened by the **chair** – the person who controls the meeting and decides who will speak and when. To start the meeting, the chair reads out the **motion** to be debated. The motion is the viewpoint which people will argue for or against. It is presented in a formal way which begins: 'This house believes that …'

The debate begins with a speech in favour of the motion. The person who speaks first in favour of the motion is called the **proposer**.

Then there is a speech against the motion by a person called the **opposer**.

The chair then declares the motion **open to the floor**. This means that anyone in the audience may now speak either for or against the motion. Anyone who wishes to speak raises their hand, and the chair asks them to speak in turn.

There are then two further speeches – one in favour of and one against the motion. The people who give these speeches are called **seconders**.

After a suitable time to allow as many people as possible to express their views, the chair invites the main speakers to **sum up**. The opposer gives a summary of the main arguments why people should vote against the motion, and the proposer gives a summary of the main arguments why they should vote for the motion.

A **vote** is then organised. The chair reads out the motion and asks 'all those in favour' to raise their hands. They are counted, and then 'all those against' are asked to raise their hands. After they are counted, the chair asks those who wish to **abstain** to raise their hands and the abstentions are counted. (You may wish to abstain for a number of reasons, either because you cannot make up your mind or because you do not agree with either of the views people have expressed.)

Organise your own debate

Either choose your own motion or organise a debate on one of these motions:

1 This house believes that all animals have the right to die naturally.

2 This house believes that children should be allowed to wear what they like to school.

3 This house believes that the monarchy is out of date and should be abolished.

The chair announces the **result** of the vote and declares that the motion has 'been carried' or 'passed' (the house agrees with motion) or 'defeated' (the house disagrees with the motion).

TIPS ON WRITING A SPEECH

✎ **Grab their attention** *Make sure you start with a statement or question that will capture the audience's attention. For* example: 'What's wrong with eating meat? 90% of us do. So why should we feel guilty?'

✎ **Use facts and statistics** *Support your statements with statistics and examples. This strengthens your arguments. For example:* 'As many as 90% of battery hens are unable to walk properly.'

✎ **Include lists of three** *Statements which list things in threes are more likely to hold the audience's attention and stick in their minds. For example:* 'Vegetarianism is cruelty-free, environmentally friendly and healthy.'

✎ **Use alliteration** *A statement which includes a number of words starting with the same letter is likely to be more memorable. For example:* 'It's time to stop the senseless slaughter.'

✎ **Refer to personal experiences** *This suggests you really know what you are talking about. For example:* 'I've seen pictures of calves, only a few days old ...'

✎ **Include questions** *These can have a dramatic effect, particularly if they are questions that do not require an answer (these are called rhetorical questions). For example:* 'Isn't it obvious that a meat-free diet is better?'

✎ **Involve the audience** *Addressing the audience directly can help to get them on your side. For example:* 'How would you like to spend your life cooped up in a cage?'

✎ **'Set them up and knock them down'** *This is a particularly effective way of undermining the opposition's arguments. For example:* 'What I can't stand about most so-called vegetarians is their hypocrisy. They claim that they don't eat meat to stop animals suffering, yet they go on eating other animal products like eggs and cheese.'

✎ **End emphatically** *Make sure you end your speech on a high note. For example:* 'Whenever you eat meat you're taking the food out of someone else's mouth. If everyone in the world was to become a vegetarian, there'd be enough food for everybody.'

Writing a speech

There are a number of techniques you can use when writing a speech in order to make it more effective. The advice above is from a helpsheet which a teacher gave to a class who were going to debate the motion 'This house believes that people who aren't vegetarians are selfish and cruel.'

◑ In pairs

Research the topic, to find out the facts and what the arguments are for and against the issue that is being debated. Then form your opinions. Tell each other which side of the argument you support and draft your speech.

Show your speech to your partner and each make any suggestions you can think of to improve it.

Some young people enter into sexual relationships and have sex without thinking about the consequences. The aim of this unit is to make you aware of what is involved in having a sexual relationship and of the steps you can take to avoid an unwanted pregnancy and to avoid catching a sexually transmitted infection.

Sex and Contraception ...
Your Questions Answered

1 What is the right age to have sex?

In Britain it is illegal for a boy to have sex with a girl under the age of 16.

We all know that some girls are very mature at 16 and some are still years away from forming serious relationships. The choice and risks are yours to take, but what's revealing is that the more teenagers know about sex and relationships, the longer they wait to make love. Young people in Holland (who are usually given frank sex education from an early age and find it easier than us Brits to talk openly with parents and teachers) start having sex an average of two years after we do.

Make up your own mind, don't bow to peer pressure and get all the facts and info you need to make informed and safe decisions about your own sex life – then you'll know when the time is right.

2 Who should I talk to about contraception?

The first person you should speak to is the person you're planning to have sex with. This should be something he has to worry about too. If you're counting on acting as a couple then you should sort out contraception together. That could mean he comes along to the doctor's with you to lend a bit of support or maybe he's the one who buys the condoms.

3 What if I'm underage and I want contraceptive advice?

Most doctors will be understanding about what you want and will treat your case in confidence. You can double check about confidentiality beforehand if you don't want your parents to know that you need birth control (see question 4). What you'll find is that most medical staff would rather see you taking a sensible view towards contraception than coming in a few months later asking for a pregnancy test.

4 Can my doctor tell my parents I'm having sex?

This is still very much up to the individual doctor, but most GPs now agree that young people under 16 can see them for contraceptive advice without parental consent. If you are not sure your doctor offers this service then you can phone reception and ask if he or she will give under-16s this sort of treatment. If you don't feel confident enough to go there then try making an appointment at a family planning clinic or at Brook.

5 Is the pill foolproof?

The pill is one of the most reliable forms of contraception, but only if you follow the instructions on the enclosed leaflet very carefully. If you skip pills or vary the times when they are taken then you may reduce the effectiveness.

Contraceptive injections are another method that some more forgetful pill-takers are turning to. They are given a painless injection in their backside every 12 weeks and are protected until their next appointment at the clinic.

6 What is emergency contraception?

Some people still refer to emergency contraception as the morning-after pill, which is confusing because it can be taken up to 72 hours after unprotected sex has taken place. If you think you need emergency contraception, make an appointment with your doctor or phone a clinic.

contraception and safer sex

Natural methods of preventing unwanted pregnancies

As Anita Naik explains, the trouble with natural methods of avoiding an unwanted pregnancy is that they are either unsuitable for teenagers or not reliable.

The rhythm method

This works on the principle that there are certain days within your cycle when you can have sex without getting pregnant. It's not suitable for young people because you need to have extremely regular periods to work out your fertile and infertile days. It also means you have to plan sex. On top of all this, this method does not protect you from HIV and STIs (sexually transmitted infections).

Withdrawal

Not a reliable form of contraception. Withdrawal is when a boy removes his penis from a girl's vagina before he ejaculates. It's a useless method because sperm can and does leak out before ejaculation. It's impossible to control this – so don't believe any boy who says he can stop it happening.

I'm worried about protection

'I'm 13 and I'm going steady with a boy. Last weekend we were in his bedroom and we ended up on the bed. We would have gone all the way if I hadn't said I had my period. I'm very worried about contraception. I overheard him talking to his best mate saying that we were going to have sex and that we didn't need to use contraception. I don't know what to do. I'm scared to say anything, but I don't want to end up pregnant.'

Tricia Kreitman says:

Having sex without a condom or any other form of contraception means one thing – you get pregnant, probably quite quickly. I don't think you should have sex with him at all. This boy's a real idiot and he's bragging to his friends that he's going to get you into bed. Presumably he sees not wearing a condom as some kind of macho statement, whereas in reality it's stupidity and cowardice.

I'm sorry but I think you're both too young to have sex and the very fact you can't discuss contraception illustrates this. Legally you're still three years under the age of consent and, if he's older than you, he could get into real trouble.

But more important, I can see that you are likely to get hurt. I don't think this boy's worth the bother because he sees you as a trophy or something to brag about rather than someone he's in love with. Please give it more time and don't do anything that you'll regret.

From 'Your Top 50 Problems Solved', *MIZZ*

How can I avoid AIDS?

AIDS breaks down the immune system, so the body loses the ability to fight off disease and infection. It's caused by the HIV infection which can be passed through sexual contact and the exchange of bodily fluids (like semen, vaginal secretions and blood). That means that unprotected vaginal and anal sex is of particular risk and this is the most common way that the virus is spread.

Sexually speaking, the best way to avoid AIDS in the modern world is to decide not to sleep with anyone. But if that's not realistic for you then it's essential you protect yourself by using a condom every time you have sex. You can't catch anything from sharing cutlery or cups, sitting on the same toilet seat as someone who's infected, or hugging.

From 50 Sex Questions Answered', *MIZZ*

✚ In groups

'Setting the age of consent at 16 is wrong.' Discuss this view. What are the arguments for and against:
a) raising the age of consent to 18;
b) lowering the age of consent to 14?

In any sexual relationship you have rights and responsibilities.

Your Sexual Rights

You have a right to enjoy sex.

When there's a lot of talk about sexual abuse, it's sometimes hard to remember that sex itself is a beautiful, natural experience – or it should be.

You have a right to wait until you're ready for sex.

One of the main ways to guarantee that you will enjoy sex is to wait until you're ready. Don't make yourself start sex before you really want to just to please a partner or keep up with the crowd.

You always have a right to say no.

Your right to say no never changes whatever the circumstances. If someone's spent money on you, taken you out, or given you presents, you don't owe him even as much as a kiss. Even if you've promised to make love and then changed your mind, you have a right to say no. Your body is not a bargaining chip and you are not for sale.

You have a right to be respected.

No one should tell you he doesn't respect you because of your sexual activities, or pressurise you because of them.

You have a right to say yes to some sexual activities and no to others.

Just because you've become physically intimate with someone doesn't mean you have to do anything you don't want. If you've almost gone all the way but haven't, you aren't obliged to. If a boy tells you that you've gone too far to stop, don't believe him.

This applies to boys too. You have as much right as anyone to stop when you want and refuse what you don't want.

Sexual rights and responsibilities

Your Sexual Responsibilities

You should always consider the feelings of your partner.

The key to a happy relationship is considering the feelings of your partner. When you are sensitive to his or her moods, likes and dislikes, you can build trust and relaxation between you. So if your partner is upset about something and wants to talk rather than kiss, put your own wishes aside for the moment and tend to his or her needs.

You should never pressurise someone to have sex.

Pressurising someone to have sex is pointless because no amount of pressure is going to create desire where there wasn't any before. If you are a boy, you should never try to force a girl to have sex with you. Even if you genuinely think a girl intends to make love and are surprised when she won't, you shouldn't pressurise her.

To use any kind of advantage or physical pressure to force a person to have sex is assault.

You should respect your partner.

Sex can make you feel vulnerable, especially when you're new to it. That is why good sexual relations require trust between the partners. If a boy or girl has told you secrets, declared love for you, or made some kind of love with you, you should never make fun of him or her for it. When people have been intimate with you like that they have made themselves vulnerable to you. Don't betray them.

You should share the responsibility for birth control and sexual health with your partner.

Part of respecting someone and being considerate of his or her feelings is being concerned over the consequences of your sexual relationship together. With the increase of sexual diseases, especially AIDS, you have a right to know if your partner is healthy. And you have a responsibility to avoid sex if you have a sexual disease.

The responsibility for birth control also belongs to both partners.

Adapted from *Stand Up for Yourself*, by Helen Benedict

Where to go for advice

What is acceptable in a sexual relationship?

⊕ In groups

People have different views about what is acceptable in a sexual relationship. On your own study the list (below) and decide which types of behaviour you think are acceptable and which are unacceptable. Then share your views in a group discussion.

1) To do things to please your boy/girlfriend.
2) To tell your friends all about what you and your partner do together.
3) To stop seeing a friend if your boy/girlfriend doesn't like them.
4) To have a relationship with someone of a different religion.
5) To lie to your parent(s) or friends about where you are going and what you are doing.
6) To have sex without being in love.
7) To tell lies to your boy/girlfriend, if you think the truth might hurt them.
8) To start having sex because one person wants to.
9) To hit each other.
10) To argue a lot.
11) To disagree about issues.
12) To go out with your friends without your boy/girlfriend.
13) To be attracted to other people while you are in a relationship.
14) To be sexually faithful to one another.
15) To let one partner take full responsibility for taking precautions.
16) To change your mind about doing something that you have made a promise to do.

Sex Myths

Everybody's doing it

Everybody's talking about it, but not everybody's doing it. If you are surrounded by friends who boast about having sex, take what they say with a pinch of salt. For starters, sex isn't something to show off about. It's a private thing between two people. Girls and boys who feel the need to tell all to everyone are usually trying to hide something.

NOT TRUE!

Having sex means you are grown-up

Sex doesn't have anything to do with being grown-up, mature or adult. In fact, lots of adults make terrible mistakes when it comes to sex. They rush into things, and live to regret it in the same way that you or I might do. Being older doesn't mean you're wiser, in the same way that doing adult things doesn't make you an adult.

NOT TRUE!

Sex strengthens a relationship

Sex only strengthens a relationship that's already strong. That means a relationship where you know and care about each other, where you've discussed things, and taken the right precautions. If you haven't done these things, sex will only weaken your relationship.

NOT TRUE!

From Wise Guides: Sex, by Anita Naik

Britain and the European Union

The European Union (EU) is a group of countries who have joined together to co-operate on economic and political issues. In 2000 there were 15 member states. The main aim of the EU is to create lasting peace and prosperity for all its citizens.

EU members 2000
Applicants for membership 2000

0   400
km

HOW IT BEGAN

The foundations of the EU were laid at the end of the Second World War (1939–45). This war was the third conflict in 70 years between two of Europe's biggest countries – France and Germany.

After the war, two Frenchmen – Jean Monnet and Robert Schuman – said there would only be lasting peace in Europe if Germany and France could learn to be friends. They decided that one way of achieving this would be to take two industries important to both countries – steel and coal – and hand over control of them to a body run by neither France nor Germany.

Other countries were also invited to join the new body when it was set up in 1951, and four did so – Italy, Belgium, Luxembourg and the Netherlands. In 1957 all six nations signed the Treaty of Rome and formed the European Economic Community (EEC). This created what is known as a Customs Union in which the six countries agreed not to put special taxes, known as tariffs, on goods imported from the other five member states.

Until this point, it was possible for Germany, for example, to put tariffs on French wine, making it dearer in German shops and therefore more difficult to sell.

Why didn't Britain join from the start?

In 1951 Britain still had strong ties with countries outside Europe. It directly controlled a number of colonies in Africa and the Caribbean, and relied on former colonies such as Australia and New Zealand for cheap food. Britain felt that its food would become more expensive and its links with colonies and former colonies would be weakened by membership of Europe. There were also fears that Britain would be giving up the right to make its own decisions.

By the 1960s, Britain changed its mind and applied to join the EEC. But the application was turned down twice by France because its president, Charles de Gaulle, thought Britain would be disruptive. However, in 1973, after de Gaulle's death, Britain did finally become a member along with the Republic of Ireland and Denmark. There was still dispute over whether our government at the time was right to make the decision, so a special vote – or referendum – was held in 1975. The whole nation voted, and around two thirds said Britain should remain part of the EEC.

From 'Gaining strength through unity', by Larry Elliott, *Guardian Education*, 26 February 1995

The development of the EU ★★★★★★★

★ **1981** Greece joins the EEC.

★ **1986** Spain and Portugal join the EEC.

★ **1987** The Single European Act is passed. Member states agree to establish a single market by the end of 1992.

★ **1992** The Maastricht Treaty is signed. Members agree to discuss future co-operation and to review their political, economic and cultural links. A decision is made to introduce a single currency (see page 79) by the beginning of 1999. But the UK negotiated an 'opt-out' clause allowing it to decide whether to join at a later stage.

★ **1993** The single market is set up. The EEC becomes the EU.

★ **1995** Austria, Finland and Sweden join the EU.

★ **1997** The Treaty of Amsterdam is signed. Job creation is made a top priority. It is agreed to make preparations for the EU to be enlarged (see page 78) and to review how the EU is working.

★ **1999** The single currency is introduced.

The Single Market

By 1 January 1993, the then 12 EU countries were part of a Single Market where they could exchange goods without long and expensive delays at the frontiers and make it easier for people to move around to other countries – this is often called the free movement of goods, capital, services and people.

The idea is that companies can buy, sell and invest in any EU country without having to go through checks, pay VAT in each country or go through long and expensive import/export formalities at the frontier – saving a lot of time, red tape and money. This also means that more and more products are available from all round the EU in our shops, and at cheaper prices.

From What Exactly Is Europe?, by Muriel Lamb

⊕ In groups

Discuss how the EEC was set up and why Britain did not join until 1973.

Explain what the Single Market is and what advantages there are for the EU countries which belong to it.

⊕ In groups

What do you see as the advantages and disadvantages of Britain's membership of the European Union? Are you for or against continued membership of the EU? Give your reasons.

Organise a debate on the motion: 'This house believes that Britain should withdraw from the EU.'

Should Britain remain in the EU?

Since the UK joined the EEC in 1973 there has been an on-going debate about whether it should remain a member.

The three main political parties have different attitudes to Europe. The most pro-European party are the Liberal Democrats who are in favour of the European Union forging even closer political ties. The Labour Party wants Britain to be fully involved in the running of the European Union and at the heart of Europe. The Conservative Party is sceptical about Britain's future in Europe and wants Britain to be 'in Europe, but not run by Europe'.

Supporters
Supporters of the European movement argue that the UK's trade with Europe has grown enormously since the UK joined the EEC. 59% of UK exports are sold to other EU countries.

Withdrawing from the EU would have a dramatic impact on our trade. It could affect our economy to such a degree that people's standard of living might fall.

They also point to the fact that you can travel freely within EU countries, with few of the border controls that other countries have in place. Also, any citizen of Europe can work in any of the member states.

Critics
Critics of the EU argue that the EU is wasteful and inefficient. They point out that about £1 billion a year (1.4% of the EU budget) is lost through fraud. They argue that Britain would be just as prosperous economically if more of its trade was done with other countries, such as the USA and the countries of the Commonwealth.

Opponents of the EU say that too many decisions are taken in Brussels rather than in London. For example, they are strongly opposed to proposals that taxation in EU countries should be harmonised. They say that belonging to the EU undermines Britain's national sovereignty, because European law has supremacy over national law.

How does the EU affect you?

Being a citizen of the EU makes it easier for you to travel, study or work in Europe. It also protects your rights, your health and your safety and helps to provide you with a good standard of living.

Your standard of living

 As a European citizen you should enjoy a higher standard of living. The 15 countries in the EU work together to develop their economies so that people in all the member states will benefit. For example, money is given to projects in the poorer regions so that companies can make a profit and create jobs. In your area you might see a new bridge, a new motorway or a new business centre being built. EU money is given to regions where there is industrial decline, rural depopulation and high unemployment to pay for the development of the infrastructure.

Your human rights

 The European Union is committed to the elimination of racism and other forms of discrimination both within its borders and throughout the world.

The EU also supports equal opportunities for women. The 1997 Treaty of Amsterdam expressly banned discrimination on grounds of sex in all member states.

The European Commission on Human Rights exists to see that human rights are upheld in all EU countries. If you feel that your human rights have been violated, you can write to the Commission. It will then decide whether to pass your case to the European Court of Human Rights.

Your career opportunities

 Special programmes provide opportunities for you to travel, study and/or gain work experience in another member state. Under EU rules the qualifications you gain in one country must, in general, be recognised in other countries. You also have the right to receive the same job opportunities, terms and conditions of employment, or to set up a business anywhere in the EU.

Your rights as a consumer

 Your rights as a consumer are protected by a set of rules that apply to shops throughout the EU. For example, foods must be clearly labelled to show their ingredients and how much they weigh and measure.

Items such as toys and electrical goods have to meet very strict safety regulations. Those which have passed the tests are marked with the CE mark.

You can buy goods produced in EU countries without having to pay the extra costs or duty that is usually put on things which are imported from other countries. This gives you more choice at reasonable prices.

Your right to travel

 Being a citizen of the EU makes it easier to travel abroad. Your burgundy coloured European passport makes it easy to cross borders and you can go through the 'blue exit' at ports and airports, without having to make any declaration to customs, provided that you are carrying only goods for your personal use.

If you are ill while you are in a member state, you can receive medical attention just as you would at home. You simply have to fill in a form called an E111 which you can obtain from your nearest main post office, before you go abroad.

EUROPEAN COMMUNITY
UNITED KINGDOM OF GREAT BRITAIN AND NORTHERN IRELAND

PASSPORT

✦ In groups

Discuss what you learn from this page about how being a citizen of Europe affects you. What effect do you think it would have on you if Britain were to withdraw from the EU?

What is being done by the EU to protect the environment?

Your environment

The EU has been developing a series of Environmental Action Programmes, and more than 200 laws have been agreed. These are designed to make the environment in which you live safe and healthy.

⊕ In groups

List and discuss all the measures that Europe has taken so far to protect the environment. Suggest other things that you think the EU should do in order to protect the environment.

To combat air pollution EU rules have been set to reduce the level of pollutants coming out of vehicle emissions and industrial factories and encourage the use of lead-free petrol. The EU is promoting public transport, as this is more environmentally friendly, and 'car-free cities'. Projects in Bath and Leicester are looking at ways of removing private cars from city centres to reduce pollution.

EU rules also set out minimum water quality standards for the treatment of drinking water to ensure that the water we drink is good for human health. As for surface waters, such as lakes, rivers, canals and groundwaters (springs), these are monitored carefully under EU laws. EU rules also ensure that bathing waters and waters for shellfish and freshwater fish are clean. EU rules protect against the discharge of dangerous substances into waters. When you go on holiday look out for the European Blue Flag for beaches. This is an award given to the cleanest beaches around Europe.

Other action includes measures to reduce noise emissions from motor vehicles, aircraft, tractors and lawnmowers, and to protect workers from noise at the workplace.

The EU encourages the safe disposal and reuse of waste, especially nuclear materials, and safety measures for the transport of chemicals and other dangerous substances.

Money is given to carry out research in many areas, for example, monitoring natural disasters, changes in the ozone layer, the production of safe, renewable energy sources (such as solar energy and windmills) and nuclear safety.

The EU has launched an initiative which enables consumers to know whether the products they buy are bad for the environment. When you buy a washing machine or dishwasher, for example, you should look for the 'ECO-label' which tells you which products cause least damage to the environment.

Farmers are being encouraged to use fewer pesticides and fertilisers and to use agricultural production methods which preserve the countryside.

Money is given to local and regional organisations in designated areas of conservation. The UK has taken the lead in setting up Environmentally Sensitive Areas – this means, for example, protecting and developing wetland nature reserves, natural habitats and European wildlife and forests.

Other regional projects encourage the development of 'green tourism' – to attract tourists while also improving the environment – for example, by creating cycle routes through the countryside.

For big projects – like the building of a new motorway or bridge – the builders now have to assess first how their project will affect the environment. This is called an Environmental Impact Assessment.

Adapted from *What Exactly Is Europe?*, by Muriel Lamb

WASTE WATER DISPOSAL SCHEME
CONTRACT NO.2
NORTH BANK AND SOUTH BANK
INTERCEPTOR SEWERS

CIVIL ENGINEERING CONTRACTOR:
ROGERS

PATK. J. TOBIN & CO.,
CONSULTING ENGINEERS,
GALWAY & DUNDALK.

JOHN DINEEN B.E.,C.Eng., M.I.E.I.
BOROUGH ENGINEER
CORPORATION OF DROGHEDA

THIS PROJECT HAS RECEIVED 85% FINANCIAL ASSISTANCE FROM THE COHESION FUND OF THE EUROPEAN COMMUNITIES

How is the European Union run?

The EU is run by five main institutions which, together with the European Council, make, interpret and monitor the laws of the European Union.

The European Council is a summit meeting of the heads of government of each member state. It usually meets twice a year to discuss policy and give overall direction to the EU's programme.

European institutions

Each of the five main institutions has representatives from the 15 member states. So EU policies and decisions are made by UK representatives acting in consultation with representatives from the countries which are our partners in the EU.

The Council of Ministers

This is the EU's main decision-making body. It consists of one government minister from each member state. They discuss proposals for new laws put forward by the European Commission and ensure that national interests are considered. The Council is based in Brussels and each country takes a turn at holding its presidency, which changes every six months. In 2000 the presidency was shared between Portugal (January to June) and France (July to December). Sweden and Belgium share the presidency in 2001 and Spain and Denmark in 2002.

The European Court of Auditors

Its role is to monitor the financial management of the EU and to look after the interests of the EU's taxpaying citizens by checking that the EU's money is actually being used for the purposes for which it is intended. It also assists the European Parliament in checking the budget each year. The Court has 15 members, one for each country.

The European Commission

There are 20 commissioners, who are appointed by the governments of the member countries. There are two commissioners from each of the larger member states (France, Italy, Germany, the UK and Spain) and one from each of the other ten countries. Each commissioner has responsibility for a particular area of policy. Once they have been appointed, commissioners are expected to act independently in the interests of all member states.

The Commission is based in Brussels and has three main functions: 1) it proposes new laws; 2) it makes sure EU treaties and other measures are implemented by member states; 3) it oversees the administration of the EU.

The European Parliament

This meets in Strasbourg and consists of 626 members who are elected from the 15 member states. Elections are held every five years in June and the next elections are in 2004. Members of the European Parliament are known as MEPs and there are 87 MEPs from the UK.

MEPs have considerable powers. They are consulted on proposals for new laws, give their opinions, suggest amendments and in some cases make decisions jointly with the Council of Ministers, especially with regard to the budget (see page 77). The European Parliament can also dismiss the European Commission, if it feels that it is not operating as it should be.

The European Court of Justice

This sits in Luxembourg and there are 15 judges, one from each member state. Its role is to interpret European laws and to decide whether actions are against European law. It has the power to rule against national governments which are breaking European laws. However, the European Court of Justice has no power to overturn decisions of British courts.

⊕ In groups

Discuss what you learn from this page about the institutions of the European Union. Where do you think the real power lies in the EU?

How European laws are made

The Commission forwards a proposal for a new EU law to the European Parliament.

The European Parliament discusses it, and perhaps amends it, then passes it back to the Commission.

The Commission drafts a firm proposal, which is sent to the European Council.

The Council makes suggestions and amendments, consulting their national parliaments. It then adopts a 'common position' on the proposal.

The 'common position' is considered by the European Parliament.

If the European Parliament approves, the Council adopts the proposal. Even if the Parliament rejects the proposal, the Council can adopt it as long as it is a unanimous decision.

EU regulations automatically become law in all member states. The EU can also pass 'directives' which tell member states to introduce a new law within a time limit.

In groups

Discuss what you learn from this page about **a)** how European laws are made, and **b)** how the EU raises money and how it spends it. Do you think that large rich countries, such as the UK and Germany, should support smaller poorer countries, such as Ireland and Portugal, to develop their economies?

The Lowry Arts Centre, Salford Quays, in the former Manchester docks. With the help of the European Regional Development Fund, the Salford Quays have been transformed into a commercial, cultural and tourist centre, creating 4,000 jobs.

The EU budget

How the income and expenditure of the European Union is distributed

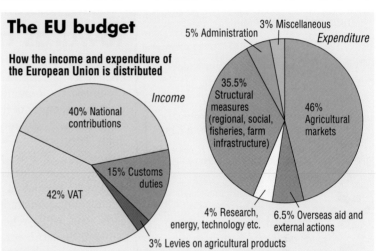

Income
- 40% National contributions
- 42% VAT
- 15% Customs duties

Expenditure
- 5% Administration
- 3% Miscellaneous
- 35.5% Structural measures (regional, social, fisheries, farm infrastructure)
- 46% Agricultural markets
- 4% Research, energy, technology etc.
- 6.5% Overseas aid and external actions
- 3% Levies on agricultural products

When countries join the EU, their governments agree to give some of their revenue to European Union institutions, which then redistribute the money on common actions. The European Commission draws up a preliminary draft budget each year, which is then amended or adopted by the Council of Ministers and the European Parliament.

The EU collects VAT charged on goods and services by the member states in their countries. About 40% of the EU's income comes from VAT. A further 40% comes from national contributions. Some countries, such as the UK and Germany, are called 'net contributors', because they contribute more to the EU budget than they take out. Other countries, such as Ireland, Greece and Portugal, receive larger amounts of money than they contribute, in order to help them to develop their economies. About 15% of EU revenue comes from customs duties which are collected on goods imported from non-EU countries.

Developing the European Union

Any country in Europe can apply to join the EU. There are 13 countries which have submitted applications to join the EU (see map on page 72). Countries which apply to join the EU must meet certain requirements:

- Their system of government must be democratic.
- They must respect human rights.
- They must have a market economy that operates in the same way as the economies of existing EU member countries.

Enlargement

Many people are in favour of increasing the size of the EU. They argue that the larger the market, the more opportunities there would be for trade and that all member states would benefit. They say that it would further help to preserve peace. It would protect the people in the countries which join by guaranteeing their human rights and helping them to develop their democratic systems of government. A larger Europe would also be able to have more influence and play a bigger part in world affairs.

Opponents argue that increasing the size of the EU will make it much harder for the EU to operate. Already there are difficulties in reaching decisions on controversial issues, such as the single currency, where member states may have different views. European institutions would have to be reformed. There would have to be more co-operation and compromise, with many more decisions taken on a majority basis rather than unanimously.

Towards a Federal Europe?

Some politicians, such as the President of the European Commission, Romano Prodi, want the members of the EU to develop much closer political links. They want to see taxes harmonised and a common foreign policy adopted. They think the EU should develop into a political union, in which each state, while retaining its national government, would increasingly operate as one of a federation of states in a 'United States of Europe'.

At present, member states retain the right to veto proposals on many key issues, such as taxation and matters of foreign policy. Those in favour of a federal Europe want member states to agree to give up the veto which they see as hindering reform and integration of the union.

Anti-federalists see closer political union as a threat to national sovereignty and national identity. They do not want to see the European Union become too powerful and fear that it could become dominated by the countries with the strongest economies. They think that in such a large political body individual citizens would have too little influence and that there would be too much bureaucracy and centralisation. They argue that the veto should be retained in many areas including taxation, defence, social security, border controls, the EU's budget mechanisms and treaty changes.

⊞ In groups

'Any European country which applies for membership and meets the criteria should be accepted into the EU.' Say why you agree or disagree with this view.

Discuss the arguments for and against a federal Europe.

The single currency

The idea of the single currency is to have one currency for countries within the EU. The aim is to make it easier and less costly for businesses to do trade. When you have different currencies, you have to pay something every time you change your money into another currency. Transferring money also takes time and causes delays. Besides, you can never be sure how much your money is going to be worth from day to day, as the rate of exchange varies.

The single currency, known as the **euro**, was introduced in 1999. Eleven countries joined the euro (making the euro zone): Germany, France, Italy, Spain, Netherlands, Belgium, Austria, Finland, Portugal, Ireland and Luxembourg. The British government decided not to join because it did not consider that the economic circumstances were right. It therefore delayed making a final decision on whether or not Britain should join.

Until 2002 the euro will exist alongside the various different national currencies. On 1 January 2002 euro notes and coins will start circulating. All national currencies, such as the franc and the mark, will be phased out and replaced by the euro within the first six months of 2002.

Should Britain join the euro?

YES

✔ Once euro notes and coins start circulating, it will no longer be necessary to exchange pounds for other currencies when going on holiday in the euro zone. At the moment we have to pay a bank every time we exchange money – if you start off with £100 and travel to four or five countries, changing it into different currencies each time, you can end up with just £70 without spending anything.

✔ Having the same currency will also mean we will be able to understand the exact amount we are spending when abroad. Instead of going into a shop in France, for example, and having to mentally convert francs into pounds, the price tag will be in euros.

✔ The prices on some expensive goods – especially cars – vary considerably across Europe, and are often more expensive in Britain. A single currency would expose price differences (often amounting to thousands of pounds) and force retailers to cut their prices in order to compete.

✔ Many overseas companies based in Britain sell goods to the rest of Europe – such as Kodak and Toyota. If Britain stays out of the euro, some might move abroad leaving thousands jobless here.

✔ We don't want to be left out – or behind. The euro zone countries are likely to form a powerful economic and political alliance from which Britain would be excluded. This would mean Britain having less influence over decisions made by the European Union which directly affect our everyday lives.

NO

✘ Joining the euro is a once-and-for-all step. There is no going back. It would mean abolishing the pound for ever.

✘ Although the Government says it will judge whether Britain should join on economic grounds, it is also very much a political decision. Do we really want to be part of a process that could eventually lead to a single European country – a 'United States of Europe'? Or do we want to retain our national identity and independence?

✘ Britain is the fifth largest economy in the world and is shortly expected to overtake France and take fourth place. It could survive on its own quite comfortably without being part of a single currency zone. The United States and Japan do business with the European Union and have their own currencies. Britain could survive the same way.

✘ Europe sells more to Britain than it buys – so it would certainly not be to their advantage to shut Britain out of a so-called single market.

✘ The argument that British interest rates (the extra amount we have to pay for borrowing money) will be lower inside the euro zone might be true if we joined tomorrow but would not always be the case. Interest rates could go up just as Britain needs them to come down and vice versa.

✘ Since the euro began operating in the 11 countries, we've already seen that the currency is not as stable as its supporters suggest.

✘ The euro is, at the end of the day, an experiment, so no one knows whether it will work or not. Does Britain really want to risk being involved with an irreversible economic 'guinea pig'?

⊕ In groups

From an article by Philip Johnston, *The Daily Telegraph*, 26 June 1999

Do you think Britain should join the euro? Discuss the arguments for and against Britain joining the single currency.

for your file

Write a letter to a newspaper or magazine stating your views on the single currency issue.

The school environment

> " It doesn't matter what the school looks like, it's only a school. "
>
> " The appearance of the school and grounds is important. They create the atmosphere of the school. "
>
> " It's up to everyone to look after the school and make sure the environment is pleasant. "
>
> " It's up to the local council to look after the school. "
>
> " People put up with things about the school environment that they'd never put up with in their own homes. "
>
> " Schools are like all public places. The environment suffers because people don't see it as their responsibility. "

 In groups

Discuss these comments about the school environment. How much do you think the school environment matters? Why do people put up with things at school that they wouldn't put up with at home? Whose responsibility is it to look after the school environment?

An environmental survey

Carry out a survey of the condition of the school's buildings and grounds. Draw up a chart like the one below and rate the condition of each area as either Good, Fair or Bad.

Area	Condition		
	Good	Fair	Bad
School gates/signs	☐	☐	☐
School drives/pathways	☐	☐	☐
School grounds/yards	☐	☐	☐
Playing fields	☐	☐	☐
Entrance hall	☐	☐	☐
Corridors	☐	☐	☐
Staircases	☐	☐	☐
Noticeboards	☐	☐	☐
Assembly hall	☐	☐	☐
Dining room	☐	☐	☐
Science labs	☐	☐	☐
Technology rooms	☐	☐	☐
Art room	☐	☐	☐
Music block	☐	☐	☐
Gymnasium	☐	☐	☐
Toilets	☐	☐	☐
General classrooms	☐	☐	☐

 In groups

1 Show each other your surveys and discuss your views of the condition of the different areas of the school. Choose three areas which you would select as priority areas for improvement and share your ideas in a class discussion.

2 Imagine that it has been announced that schools can bid for up to £25,000 of lottery money for projects to improve the school environment. Discuss ideas for projects to improve your school environment. Choose one and draft a proposal to put to the rest of the class. Debate the various proposals, then vote to choose what your class's project would be.

3 Talk about what you could do to improve the appearance and atmosphere of your tutor group room. Organise a working party to investigate what any suggested improvements might cost and, if necessary, approach the appropriate school committee to apply for funds or hold a fundraising event. Then carry out the improvements. At the same time, to ensure that the tutor group room is always kept tidy and attractive, organise a weekly rota of monitors with responsibility for keeping the classroom tidy and the noticeboards neat.

The local environment

Wherever you live, your environment is important. Each day you make choices which have an effect on the environment. Taking action about the environment starts with doing things in your everyday life that help to cut down on waste, to conserve resources and to preserve the environment.

Local Agenda 21
Changing the way we live

What is Local Agenda 21?

Local Agenda 21 is a challenge for individuals, communities, businesses (in fact everyone) to get out, get active and get involved in changing the way we live at the moment.

Although the Earth is large, we are using up its resources faster than they can be replaced. We are polluting air, water and soil; we are creating more and more waste and destroying our environment in many ways.

In 1992 the UN conference on Environment and Development (the Earth Summit) was held in Rio, Brazil. One of the outcomes was Agenda 21, an action programme for sustainable development, signed by 179 nations including the UK.

It is not a fixed law, but an agreement between governments that they will promote sustainable development. Some of the topics included in Agenda 21 were promoting energy efficiency, preventing pollution, protecting endangered areas and reducing our consumption of the world's resources.

Local Agenda 21 is an initiative by local councils to get people involved in changing the way they live in order to promote sustainable development.

What is sustainable development?

Sustainable development means meeting our present needs without compromising the ability of future generations to meet their needs. It means making progress and improving the quality of our life without destroying the planet or having a bad effect on other people in the process.

To have a sustainable lifestyle we have to consider the resources we use, whether we are producing too much waste, how much pollution we produce, and how we affect the natural environment.

How can you become involved?

Local Agenda 21 challenges everyone to take responsibility for the problems the Earth is facing.

You can start by doing small things in your life towards sustainable living, such as turning the tap off when you clean your teeth, buying locally grown foods or recycling your cans and paper.

There may be a bigger project that you can become involved in, either by volunteering or taking part in a project organised by your school. There are many Local Agenda 21 projects that have been successful throughout the country (see pages 82–83).

From *The Local Agenda 21 Handbook*, 1999

⊕ In groups

On your own, make lists of things you can do individually to help save energy, cut down on waste and reduce pollution. Then compare your ideas in a group discussion.

Making a difference – changing places

Young people throughout the UK are making a difference to the environment by getting involved in projects organised by their schools, local councils and organisations such as the environmental charity Groundwork.

Groundwork works in partnership with the government, councils, businesses and communities. It is the UK's leading environmental regeneration charity, active in 150 towns and cities, developing projects that link environmental, social and economic regeneration.

Groundwork encourages young people to participate in making decisions about how to improve the local environment by getting them to identify needs and put forward proposals.

I value my valley

Groundwork Bridgend's GreenIT programme helped children in the Garw Valley use information technology to assess community needs and prepare planning guidelines. The result? The Garw Green Guide, a unique reference handbook for planners. Joanne Webb (13), a Year 8 student from Ynysandre Comprehensive School, explains:

'We looked at Pontycymer village square – there's just a bus shelter and a couple of shops. We wanted to make it a bright and interesting place to go. We did a survey of local people, then gathered materials, took photos and made sketches.

We got ideas from different architects, animals, nature, mining and sport. We drew pictures and made models out of clay, papier mâché and scrap materials.

We suggested different kinds of benches and railings, maybe a monument and renovating the bus shelter. We didn't want very bright colours, because if they were too bright, they just wouldn't have gone with the trees and grass. For the monument we made big models of a rugby player and a runner.

Using a computer design package we made graphs of what people wanted, and of the colours. Finally we went down to the council chambers and did a presentation to the mayor. It was pretty nerve-wracking but we knew what we had to do!'

From *Groundwork Today*, issue 2

Giving young people a voice

Mary Donkin (15) took part in 'Young Voices Durham', a project which enabled young people to express their views.

'Groundwork explained about Local Agenda 21. I hadn't heard of it before. I was interested in the environment but this made me more interested. People usually don't want to listen to what young people have to say about anything, they just go ahead and do things, and that's not what we want.

I think with Young Voices, if we can show that we care first, through doing little things to start with – for one thing we need a lot more litter bins in our village – if we can do that, then we can work our way up and change the major things. We're learning more about making ourselves heard.'

In groups

Investigate your local environment to identify what you think might be done to improve it. Use your IT skills to design a questionnaire which surveys people's opinions, to analyse the results and to draft a proposal. Either send a copy of your proposal to the local newspaper or invite a local councillor to come to the school to discuss your ideas.

Change on the Estate

A lack of leisure and recreation facilities was a key problem identified by young people on the Sholver Estate in Oldham. As part of Groundwork's Young Leaders programme, a group of young people worked alongside Groundwork Rochdale, Oldham and Tameside to revitalise a dilapidated children's play area and create a landscaped seating area in front of the local community centre.

As a follow-up to this project, the Young Leaders also campaigned for, and helped to provide, the estate's first sports area – one which would be accessible to the whole community.

From *Old Problems, Young Solutions*, a Groundwork leaflet

To mark the new millennium, Groundwork participated in the 'Trees of Time and Place' project in which people across the UK planted 'personal trees'. The picture shows young people from the Nottingham Sikh Youth Group who took part in the project.

In groups

Organise your own MADD event to take place for two to three hours one evening after school or on a Saturday morning.

First, make a list of the different things you could do to help the local community in the time available. Share your ideas in a class discussion. Draw up a class list of jobs and get people to volunteer for them. Appoint a committee of four or five people to act as a steering group to plan the event and to make sure that everyone involved knows what is expected of them.

After the event discuss how it went, talk about what went well and what you would do differently when organising a similar event in the future.

Go MADD

ORGANISE A MAKE A DIFFERENCE DAY

Make a Difference Day (MADD) is an annual event, usually a Saturday in October, organised by Community Service Volunteers, 237 Pentonville Road, London N1 9NJ. Thousands of people throughout the UK donate a few hours of their time to help the local community in some way, for example by cleaning graffiti off a bus shelter, cleaning up the local pond or doing some shopping for an older person.

for your file

Write a press release to send to your local paper explaining how you organised your Make a Difference Day and what people did.

Attitudes towards older people

Ageism

To be old in Britain today is considered by many to be 'past it', 'over the hill' or a 'has been'.

Such attitudes towards older people are widespread in a society such as ours which values youth, beauty and material possessions.

For many people, who are not old themselves, growing old is something to be feared. It is seen as a time of loss and withdrawal from life, rather than as a natural development which occurs gradually over time. Yet if you were to ask older people how they feel about being 'old', they are likely to respond by saying that although they may look old, they still feel young inside.

Many of the negative images we have about older people are perpetuated by the media, which tends to portray them as victims of crime, poverty or neglect, or as figures of fun. To judge a person negatively simply because they are old is ageist.

Once you become aware of it, however, ageism is apparent in all areas of life – from the derogatory way we refer to older people as 'geriatrics', 'old fogies', or 'wrinklies' to the patronising way we treat older people as if they are children and need protecting. It also shows itself in the embarrassment and condemnation we express if an older person continues to have an interest in sex or if they prefer to dress in a style which we think is inappropriate for their age.

Ageism is at the root of some common assumptions we make about older people – that they are all stubborn and inflexible, dependent and institutionalised, senile and sexless.

Adapted from a Help the Aged UK information pack

82 Year Old Forced To Give Up Job

An 82-year-old yoga teacher has lost her job after council officials discovered that she was too old to be employed.

For five years, Nena Joyce held four classes a week at a leisure centre before Swansea city council told her it was unable to insure her against accidents during the sessions because she was over 65.

Mrs Joyce said: 'I could understand it if I was no longer capable of doing the job, but that is not the case.'

Adapted from The Daily Telegraph, 8 March 2000

Old age and memory loss

Many people who live to be very old become forgetful. For example, they may call people by their wrong name. This is considered to be a normal part of the ageing process.

Most older people retain their full mental powers until the end of their lives. However, some older people – between 10 and 20 per cent – suffer from varying degrees of dementia.

A person who suffers from dementia gets muddled and confused because they cannot remember things. They may forget where they put things, lose track of the time or the day of the week, and confuse objects, for example, mistaking the washing machine for the fridge. A person with severe dementia may be unable to recognise people or places.

There is no single cause of dementia. Scientists are carrying out research to try to understand dementia, but until it is fully understood in many cases it cannot be treated.

⊕ In groups

Study the article on ageism (left). Discuss how people regard older people and the way that they are presented by the media. Do you think society is ageist? Appoint a spokesperson and share your views in a class discussion.

Do you think that people undervalue the contribution that older people like Mrs Joyce can make to society? Talk about older people that you know and about how they spend their time.

for your file

Write an article about the causes and effects of ageism. You could interview a number of older people and include their views in your article.

Survey finds 'two worlds of old age'

Half those aged 80 and over live on £80 a week or less according to a survey of older people's lifestyles. One in four worries about being able to afford food, while around two-thirds are concerned about paying for clothing or heating bills.

The findings are from a survey of 1,317 readers, aged 55 to over 90, of Yours, a magazine for older people.

While the majority, 90%, enjoyed retirement, a small but significant group faced a bleak old age.

The research provided evidence of 'two worlds of old age,' said the report's author, Alisoun Milne.

'If you live in your own home, in a shared household, with an occupational pension and are in the early stages of retirement, up to 75, you tend to be OK. But if you don't have that financial backing, live on your own, and are 80 or older, that tends not to be the case.'

Over half of those surveyed said they were unable to afford holidays, nearly 40% could barely buy presents, and a quarter found paying for household maintenance, heating and clothing problematic.

'Most older people enjoy retirement and contribute a great deal to their families and communities,' said Tessa Harding of Help the Aged. 'But the dire poverty of some is a real tragedy in a wealthy society.'

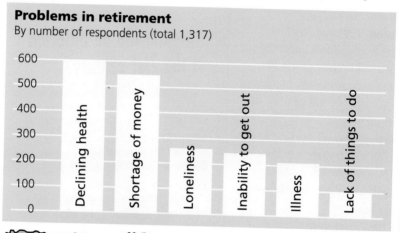

Problems in retirement
By number of respondents (total 1,317)

From an article by Sarah Hall in
The Guardian, 5 October 1999

The problems faced by older people

✛ In groups

Study the article and graph and discuss what you learn from them about the problems some older people face in old age.

Caring for older people

Many frail older people are only able to continue living in the community because they receive support from their carers and from services provided by the community, such as visiting care assistants, day care and respite care.

Older people who are frail or very disabled often cannot go out unless transport is provided for them, so transport is provided for them in special vehicles.

Once they become too frail or ill to be able to cope in their own homes, many older people have to be cared for in residential or nursing homes. Nationally, social services departments spend an average of 64% of their budget for older people on supporting residents in residential and nursing homes. However, there are limited financial resources and it is not uncommon for older people to spend a considerable time in hospital before admission to residential or nursing care.

What role should the family play?

✛ In groups

'Out of 1000 adults, 57% agreed that there was some obligation to care for older people in the family, 37% did not agree.' What role do you think the family should play in looking after older people?

What can the problems be when older people **a)** live with the family; **b)** live in their own homes? What other alternatives are there?

What can be done to support older people who live on their own and have no relatives?

An ageing population – society in the 21st century

Forecasts for the future

As the 21st century progresses there will be fewer younger people and more older people:

Between 1995 and 2040 the number of children under the age of ten will drop by nearly 20% – in the same period the number of people aged 65 will increase by over 60%.

The population of working age in the UK will drop sharply from 2011 onwards, just as the population of pensionable age rises fastest.

In 1961 there were almost four people of working age to support each pensioner; by 2040 there will be only two.

In 1951 there were 33 centenarians; in 2031 there will be 36,000.

By 2040 there will be 85% more people aged 80 and over than in 1995.

By 2040 there will be an extra 20 dependent pensioners for every 100 people of working age.

Admissions of older people to hospital are increasing by 4% a year, and over the next 35 years the proportion of people over 65 will rise by 30%.

It is projected that the number of disabled adults aged 60 and over will increase by almost 50% by 2031.

The population of pensionable age will rise to 12 million by 2021, and will peak at nearly 15.5 million around 2038.

⊕ In groups

Study the statistics in the article (left) and discuss how the age profile of society is changing.

How will life be different in the 21st century?

Young people born in the 1990s will be over 50 by the middle of the century. If you will be 50 or more in the year 2040 then the changes in society will affect you.

When the National Health Service was designed, life expectancy was around 50 years. Today it is 80 years.

By 2016 there will be almost 24 million households in Britain (23% more than in 1991) and more than one in three will consist of people living on their own.

By 2010 52% of workers will be doing some work at home. 8% of workers will be working 30 hours per week at home.

How do you think life will change because of these things?

In the 21st century, Britain will need 5 million extra homes. Do you think we should expand into the countryside to build the extra homes needed for the future?

Your retirement could last longer than your schooldays. Which do you agree with

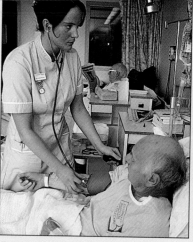

There are unlikely to be major problems in the short to medium-term future of health and care, but significant challenges could face society after 2020. Medical advances in the 21st century will mean more and more conditions can be treated. But treatment costs money. The need to ration or control health service expenditure is increasingly being debated, and there are serious risks that the needs of older people will be seen as an unacceptable cost.

– individuals should be able to choose at what age they stop working, or retirement should be compulsory in order to allow younger people to have jobs?

By 2040 there will be only two working people to support every pensioner (as opposed to four working people in 1961). Will there be pensions for people (which means YOU) in the future? Without pensions, how would old people manage?

⊕ In groups

1 What does rationing mean? How can people be given a fixed allowance of medical treatment? Would that be a fair system?

2 Should people expect medical treatment if **a)** they don't have a healthy lifestyle, **b)** they take part in dangerous sports, or **c)** they travel to countries where there are health risks?

3 Do you think people would be prepared to pay more taxes to get whatever treatment they want, when they want?

4 Can you think of a system that is fair to everyone, whatever their age?

Patrick's story

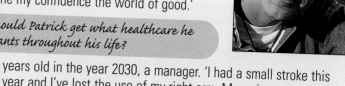

17 years old in the year 2000, a shop assistant. 'I've just had my eyes corrected with laser surgery. No more glasses for me. It's done my confidence the world of good.'

Q *Should Patrick get what healthcare he wants throughout his life?*

47 years old in the year 2030, a manager. 'I had a small stroke this year and I've lost the use of my right arm. Magazines are always going on about eating healthy foods and taking exercise, but I never took any notice. Now I wish I had.'

Q *Is it Patrick's responsibility to stay well with a healthy lifestyle?*

87 years old in the year 2070. 'My daughter's got a life of her own and I don't want to depend on her. I'm lucky I've got someone to come in and help a few hours each day. My community pays her wages. I don't know what I'd do without them, the government can't pay for everyone.'

Q *Who will Patrick want to look after him when he can't take care of himself?*

Thinking ahead

⊞ In groups

Study the stories on this page and discuss the questions and implications.

Liz's story

17 years old in the year 2000, a computer programmer. 'I'm training to be a computer programmer. I'll learn new skills as I go along, that way I've got a better chance of being employed.'

Q *How can Liz help herself to stay employed?*

47 years old in the year 2030, a project manager. 'I've started volunteering a few hours a week when I have a spell without work. They said I'd enjoy it and I can't believe how much I get out of it.'

Q *Do we value Liz's volunteer work?*

87 years old in the year 2070, still fit. 'I'm perfectly fit enough to work and I can't imagine giving it up. I do voluntary work. I'm helping myself and others at the same time.'

Q *Why should Liz retire if she doesn't want to?*

Clare's story

17 years old in 2000, a school leaver. 'I live with my mum, but I can't be bothered with her new husband and baby. I don't see much of my dad since he left; so I'm out a lot enjoying myself. After all, you're only young once.'

Q *Should Clare prefer her family or her freedom?*

47 years old in the year 2030, a mother and a secretary. 'I am very busy with my job and children. My husband already had a son when we married, he is a real handful. Thank goodness that's not my problem. Now dad is old he needs help, but I don't have time for him as well.'

Q *Should Clare be there for all her family?*

87 years old in the year 2070, a teleworker. 'I am not as mobile as I used to be, so I do telephone work from home for the local hospital. I'm determined to contribute as long as I can. In this day and age we want to be part of society whatever our age.'

Q *How can Clare be sure she is always valued?*

for your file

Write about the changes that you think you will see during your lifetime as a result of the changing age profile of society. What, if anything, do you think you need to do to prepare for them?

Most people have little idea of where their food comes from. In this article John Crace tells you some of the things that supermarkets would prefer to keep to themselves.

The foods you eat

Spoilt for choice

Walk down any supermarket aisle and you would be hard pushed to realise that 800 million people in the world do not have enough food to meet their basic nutritional needs. The shelves groan with goodies, from the bare essentials such as sugar and bread, to the outright exotic, such as star fruit and ostrich steaks, and as soon as a gap appears a stacker appears from the storeroom to restock. The choice seems bewildering and the quantities limitless.

Maintaining this illusion carries a high price for producers, consumers and the environment. Producers often barely scrape a living as supermarkets squeeze them for rock-bottom prices for their goods. Consumers are often offered foods that have been sprayed by pesticides or treated with antibiotics or other additives so that producers can maximise the return from their fields and livestock. And the environment suffers because foods are air-freighted vast distances and then wrapped in non-biodegradable packaging.

Finding foods that have neither been treated with chemicals nor boxed in plastic or polystyrene and which have been produced locally is a great deal more difficult than you might imagine, as food manufacturers want to preserve a consumer-friendly image. So product labels are not always much help. For instance, an apple pie does not have to tell you where the apples come from nor where the pie was baked. The label will not necessarily tell you if it is free of genetically modified ingredients nor, unless the pie is organically produced, will it tell you if it contains toxic pesticide residues. But the information is available; you just have to work hard to get it.

Food miles

Many British consumers have become used to eating what they want when they want. Thanks to air transport, strawberries and runner beans are now available throughout the year at leading supermarkets. But the extra costs of out-of-season foods is not just reflected in the purchase price; the environment also suffers from added airline and road freight exhaust emissions. Huge amounts of fuel are used to ship food around the world. Carbon dioxide from exhaust emissions is one of the principal causes of climate change.

Apple facts

Only 25% of dessert apples consumed in the UK are actually grown here. France, South Africa and New Zealand supply the bulk of our apples, while acres of UK orchards are bulldozed.

Pesticides

Nearly all fruit and vegetables have been grown using pesticides. There are more than 300 chemicals approved for use in the UK, and farmers spray roughly 1 billion gallons of them each year on UK crops. An apple might have received 35 pesticide treatments by the time it reaches a supermarket. In 1998, one in eight of all UK lettuces showed pesticide residues over the government's maximum level, while in 1996, one third of British milk was found to have traces of the chemical lindane.

Organic food

The term 'organic' is a legal category, enforced by the government. Any food labelled organic must be grown or reared without the use of pesticides, artificial fertilisers, genetic modification and antibiotics. Weeds and pests are controlled by natural techniques and animals are reared in humane conditions.

At present, organic farms make up 0.5% of total UK farming and 70% of organic foods sold in the UK have to be imported. It is estimated that by 2002 organic

Antibiotics

Animals reared in intensive factory farms are more likely to become ill so they are routinely dosed with antibiotics. Almost all poultry, 80% of pigs and nearly half of all sheep and cattle raised in the UK are regularly treated in this way. A 1998 Soil Association report found that farm use of tetracycline, an antibiotic widely used in human medicine, has increased 15-fold in the last 30 years. The use of penicillin-type drugs has increased sixfold.

There is increasing evidence that the overuse of antibiotics is having harmful effects on humans. The House of Lords Select Committee on Science and Technology concluded in a 1998 report that 'there is a continuing threat to human health from imprudent use of antibiotics in animals' because antibiotic residues in meat are thought to lead to resistance to antibiotics in humans, rendering the drugs ineffective in fighting human illnesses. There are already signs that some bacteria are becoming resistant to antibiotics.

food will account for 7–8% of the total UK food market, with a retail value of over £1 billion.

Organic food is usually more expensive than mass-produced food, a reflection of the extra costs of its production. Despite the cost, an increasing number of people are converting to organic food because they believe it is better for animals and the environment and is both healthier and tastes better.

GM foods

Genetic engineering allows scientists to create new plants in the laboratory. It is done by altering the genes, the vital blueprints inside all living cells that give plants and animals their different characteristics. In one experiment, a natural anti-freeze gene from a fish that allows it to survive freezing water was put into sweetcorn in an attempt to create a new type of frost-resistant sweetcorn. Most GM crops, however, are engineered to be resistant to pesticides, so that when they are sprayed on a field, everything but the crop will die.

The health effects of eating GM foods are as yet unknown, with the scientific community divided over possible risks to human health. There are also concerns that GM crops will cause genetic pollution by releasing pollen into the environment and transferring their genetic qualities to wild plants. The French government has recently placed a two-year ban on GM crops capable of pollinating with wild plants after GM oilseed interbred with wild radish and turnip to create herbicide-resistant 'super-weeds'.

Labelling of GM foods is only partially effective at present because roughly 60% of all processed foods could contain GM soya or maize, and it is not always possible to trace the origin of all ingredients.

⊕ In groups

1 Discuss what you learn from the information in this article about:
a) where our food comes from, **b)** how it is produced, and **c)** the effects that producing, packaging and transporting foods to stock our supermarket shelves have on the environment.

2 Discuss what is meant by 'organic foods'. Why are they considered by many people to be healthier than other foods? Do you think it is worth paying the extra price for organic foods?

3 What are the arguments for and against genetically modified foods? Do you think we should continue to develop them, or is the possibility that they will damage the environment too great a risk to take?

4 Discuss what you learn from the article about the problems that have resulted from giving antibiotics to animals.

5 What are your views on factory farming? Do you try to avoid eating foods that have been produced by factory farming? Is factory farming 'cruel and unnecessary'?

for your file

Write a letter to a newspaper expressing your views on one or more of the issues about the foods we eat that are raised in this article.

World hunger

" Throughout Africa food shortages are common, although more food than ever is being produced in the world. The problem is that some countries and people have more than they need while others do not have enough. " Christian Aid

Many people in the world do not get enough nourishment from the food they eat.
Malnutrition is the term used to describe lack of nutrition in a person's diet. It is estimated that almost 750 million people suffer from malnutrition – more than twice the whole population of Europe.

The causes of food shortages and famine

Famine occurs when there is an extreme shortage of food in one place. During the 1980s and 1990s there have been severe food shortages in the countries in the Horn of Africa – Ethiopia, Eritrea, Sudan and Somalia…

Drought

Drought is not the cause of famine or hunger. Often lack of rain merely tips the balance after years of hardship. There was a drought in England in 1992 but no famine because people there don't rely on their land for food.

Environmental damage

The Horn of Africa is turning into a desert. Trees have been cut down for firewood and to make room for cash crops. Trees are vital – the roots hold water and prevent the soil from being blown away. Without trees the soil becomes eroded and dry, leading to smaller and smaller harvests.

Poor land

The best land is used for cash crops for export. This has forced small farmers on to the poorer land. In Ethiopia huge state farms were set up to grow coffee. Today most of the money earned goes to repay loans from western banks, governments and organisations like the World Bank.

Poverty

Poverty is the root cause of all famines. The countries in the Horn of Africa are among the world's poorest. In 1985 parts of Sudan had a food surplus, but the government could not afford to buy it for hungry people elsewhere. Rich countries do not starve in times of drought.

Foreign debt

Loans from the World Bank and the International Monetary Fund to help Third World countries develop their economies have not helped, because of the conditions on which the loans were given. Governments must increase exports, devalue the currency and cut public spending to help repay foreign debts and balance the budget. More exports often mean less food can be produced; devaluation and cuts in subsidies mean food prices rocket; cuts in public spending mean worse health and education services.

International trade

African countries suffer from a system of international trade which benefits richer countries. Under colonialism their economies were developed to produce raw materials, like cocoa and copper, to supply industries in the West. Today many countries still depend on the same few commodities for their export earnings. In recent years, prices for these products have fallen dramatically. Too many countries are producing the same thing, so prices benefit the buyers rather than the producers. In 1985, the year of the Ethiopian famine, a collapse in world prices for raw materials meant that rich countries paid $19 million less for produce from Africa.

War

Many African countries hit by famine in 1992 were at war. But conflicts have been made much more deadly by the sophisticated weapons provided by more powerful countries. War increases the danger of famine and affects a country's ability to feed itself: crops, houses and animals are destroyed, economies are shattered and money is spent on arms instead of agriculture.

Unequal shares

According to the United Nations the average person should eat no less than 2,400 calories a day. If a person's calorie intake is constantly below that level, they are likely to suffer from malnutrition.

Most of the people who suffer from malnutrition live in the poor countries in the world's South. The world produces enough grain to provide every person with 3,000 calories a day. And that doesn't include all the beans, fruit and vegetables that are grown. The problem is that the world's food is not distributed equally.

While millions of people do not get enough to eat, people in Western Europe, North America and Japan on average eat over 25% more calories than they need. In poorer countries, the richest 10% of the population eat more than twice the number of calories eaten by the poorest 20%.

Why are they hungry?

Half the people of Sub-Saharan Africa don't have enough to eat. Here are some reasons people give.

- People in Africa are lazy.
- African countries have difficult conditions for growing food.
- There is not enough food in the world.
- People have too many children.
- Some people in the world get more than their fair share of food.
- Nothing grows in Africa, it's too hot and never rains.
- Farmers in Africa need more pesticides and fertilisers.
- African farmers are not given a fair deal in the world market.
- Drought and famine are natural disasters which cannot be prevented.
- Farmers don't have enough good land on which to grow food.

Christian Aid

Overpopulation

Many people believe that overpopulation is a major cause of famine, and in parts of Africa population growth is outstripping food production. However, the land could still produce more food. High population rates are always a symptom of poverty, *not* a cause; very poor people have a greater need for children to help them in the fields and take care of them in old age.

From 'When famine is a constant threat',

In groups

Study the information on these pages. Discuss the reasons people give for why there is hunger in Sub-Saharan Africa. Which are true? What are the real reasons why there is hunger in those countries?

for your file

Write a statement saying what you have learned from these pages about the reasons for hunger and malnutrition in some parts of the world and about how the problem could be solved.

Ten ways to beat world hunger

1 Increase the amount of aid to small farmers to help them stay on their land, for example, by giving them seeds and tools as well as food.

2 Cut down the amount of food which rich countries import from developing countries.

3 Reduce the amount of land used for growing cash crops.

4 Train farmers in methods that will increase the yield from their land.

5 Educate people so that they know which foods to grow and eat for a healthy diet.

6 Send more food aid to poor countries.

7 Introduce land reforms so that the land in developing countries is distributed more fairly.

8 Get more people in rich countries to change their eating habits, for example, by becoming vegetarians.

9 Cancel the debts which the governments of Third World countries owe to western banks.

10 Repair environmental damage and improve the quality of the land, for example, by tree-planting projects.

In groups

Discuss the ten suggestions for helping to solve the problem of world hunger. Put them in order of importance starting with the one you think will have the most long-term effect. Can you suggest other ways to help?

A person needs about 5 litres of water a day for cooking and drinking.

But to stay clean and healthy a further 25–45 litres are needed per person.

Water – a vital resource

The Water Crisis

Water is vital for all living things to survive – a few days without it and people die. In a rich country like the United Kingdom everyone has access to water. Yet for 80 countries – with 40 per cent of the world's population – lack of water is a constant threat.

Lack of water in many places in the world is an ever-worsening crisis. There is not enough water to drink and to keep crops and farm animals alive. Increases in population mean there is less water available for each person. Climate change, caused by pollution of the atmosphere, is making some countries which are already short of water even hotter and drier. Demand for water is doubling every 20 years.

The fresh clean water that is available is often wasted and misused. When people are poor they have no money to pump and pipe water. They cannot even afford proper houses. There are no sewage works to dispose of waste. As a result, what clean water there is gets mixed with dirty water and germs breed, causing illnesses. The United Nations estimates that dirty water causes 80 per cent of disease in developing countries and kills 10 million people annually. The UN believes that the lack of clean water is becoming a terrible crisis for the world. Nations may go to war to fight to control the supply of water, as they have done in the past to fight for oil.

There are ways of solving the problem. The charity Water Aid starts at the beginning, with the poor people who need the water most. These people have no access to expensive technology so all schemes are kept simple. Wells are dug and maintained with hand tools. Hand pumps can be provided so that whole villages can be supplied with clean water. Water can be brought in by pipeline and gravity does the rest.

Just as importantly, simple sewage schemes are organised so that dirty water is kept away from the clean. Many hours of work in carrying water is avoided, children stay healthy, and a huge problem gets smaller.

From 'Water water ...'

How much do you know about water?

Do this test-yourself quiz, then check the answers (see page 96).

1 How much of our bodies is made up of water?
a. 10% b. 70% c. 25%

2 What percentage of the world's population does not have access to safe, clean water?
a. 10% b. 25% c. 70%

3 How much water does it take to flush the toilet?
a. 2·5 litres b. 9·5 litres c. 19 litres

4 How much water on average does someone in the UK and Ireland use every day for drinking, washing and cooking?
a. 135 litres b. 50 litres c. 15 litres

5 Which of these diseases are caused by a lack of safe, clean water and poor sanitation?
a. dysentery b. diarrhoea c. cholera

6 How many people will die every minute in the Third World from diseases caused by unsafe water?
a. 10 b. 1 c. 30

7 Traditionally women in Africa and Asia collect the water for the whole family, carrying it up to several miles on their heads or their backs. What is the average weight of the water they carry?
a. 4 kg b. 20 kg c. 80 kg

8 How much money will provide someone in the Third World with safe water for life?
a. £2.50 b. £10 c. £50

From 'Water, water everywhere but not a drop to drink', by Paul Brown, *Guardian Education*, 18 March 1997

Life in the cities ~~~~~~

The UN estimates that 40 per cent of people in many cities do not have access to safe drinking water. People have to drink from puddles or any source they can find. Most big cities are built on rivers but because the sewers are inadequate this water is polluted. Often dirty water is pumped straight into the river.

The Yamuna River passing through the Indian capital Delhi has 200 million litres of sewage drained into it each day. This means that the thirsty poor must drink and cook with polluted water if they are to survive at all. Many know this will make them sick and so they turn to water vendors who sell tap water at huge prices. An empty Coke can of clean water can cost between 10 and 20 per cent of a poor person's income. The average person needs four of these a day to stay alive.

Women and water ~~~~~~

In many countries fetching water is women's work. Girls as young as 10 are sometimes made responsible for providing the family with water. This means walking four to five kilometres to collect it. Each litre of water weighs one kilogram and containers are often balanced on the head. The constant carrying of heavy weights can damage the neck and spine.

Many girls miss school completely because of their water-carrying duties. After wells have been dug and tap stands provided for villages, women need only take a few minutes to fetch water and children can attend school.

Water wars ~~~~~~~~~~

Most of the world's great rivers flow across continents, often through several countries. Along their banks are many cities and thousands of farmers relying on irrigation to grow crops. Each year the demand for water grows. Governments decide to dam rivers for hydroelectricity schemes or to store water for the dry season. Downstream it means people who relied on that water for their own use are deprived of it.

One of the best examples is the Nile and its tributaries which flow through seven countries. Egypt uses all the water the Nile can produce to irrigate the desert lands. Sudan, which is upstream, has agreed not to take any more. But some of the poorer countries even further inland – Eritrea, Ethiopia and Uganda – all need more water for growing populations but dare not take it. Egypt has warned them: 'Take any more and we will send in the army.'

⊕ In groups

Discuss all the ways that we use water in our homes. How would your life be different if you did not have a water supply in your home, but had to walk 4–5 kilometres to fetch your water from a stand-pipe or a well, using 10 litre containers?

Study the information on these pages and discuss what you learn from them about the problems many people in the world have of getting sufficient clean water. Why is the demand for water likely to lead to international conflicts in the future?

The carcasses of fishes killed by cyanide flowing down the Tisza river from a Romanian mine.

Assessing your progress and achievements

The aim of this unit is to help you to think about what progress you have made and what you have achieved during Year 8. It gives you the chance to discuss your progress with your tutor, to write a statement about your achievements and to look ahead and set yourself targets for what you hope to achieve in Year 9.

Your subjects

Think about the effort you have made in each of your subjects and what your progress and achievements have been.

for your file

Make a list of all the subjects you are studying and use a five-point scale to give yourself grades for effort and progress in each subject:
1 Excellent **2** Good **3** Satisfactory
4 Poor **5** Unsatisfactory.
Then write a brief comment on your work and progress in your subjects. Give reasons for the grades you have given yourself, and evidence to support your views of your progress and achievements in each subject.

Your key skills

Think about your progress in the key skills that you are learning as a result of the work which you do in your different subjects. These are the key skills:

❋ Communication skills ❋ Numeracy skills
❋ Study skills ❋ Problem-solving skills
❋ Personal and social skills ❋ ICT skills.

for your file

Think about the key skills and write a short comment on each one, saying how much you think you have improved that skill during the past year – a lot, quite a lot, only a little. Support your statement by referring to something you have done during the year.

Your activities

Think about the activities you do and what you have achieved in both school and out-of-school activities.

 In pairs

Each make a list of all the activities you have taken part in this year, both inside and outside school. Include details of events organised by clubs and societies that you belong to, sports activities, drama and musical activities and any school events that you have been involved in.

Show your list to your partner and discuss any events that were particular highlights because of what you achieved in them.

for your file

Write a short statement giving details of your most significant achievements in your activities during the year.

Your attitude and behaviour

Think about what your attitude and behaviour have been like during the year.

- Have your attendance and punctuality been good?
- Has your behaviour been good **a)** in lessons, **b)** around the school?
- Have you kept up-to-date with your work and handed it in on time?
- Have you volunteered for things and played as full a part as you could in the life of the school?

for your file

Write a short comment summing up your attitude and behaviour during Year 8.

reviewing your progress

Discussing your progress

Arrange a meeting with your tutor. Show them what you have written about your subjects and your key skills and discuss your progress and achievements in Year 8. Compare your own views with those that your teachers have made on subject reports or subject review sheets. Together decide what your strengths and weaknesses are at present.

Talk about the activities in which you have taken part and what you consider to be your significant achievements, and discuss what you wrote about your attitude and behaviour.

During the meeting listen carefully to what your tutor has to say. Add anything to your statements which your tutor thinks you have missed out. Note down any comments they make in which they disagree with your assessment, either because they think you have been too harsh on yourself, or because they think that you have overestimated the amount of progress you have made.

Recording your achievements

Use a word processor to draft a statement as a record of your progress and achievements during Year 8. Include comments on your subjects, your key skills, your activities and your attitude and behaviour.

Before you put your record in your progress file, show it to your tutor. Agree any changes that your tutor thinks you should make, so that your final statement is what you both consider to be an accurate record of your progress and achievements.

Setting targets

Use your meeting with your tutor to set targets for the future. Assessing what has gone well can help you to identify which subjects and skills you need to improve. When you have identified a subject or a skill that you need to improve, you can set yourself a target and draw up an action plan.

Making an action plan

Step 1 Decide which skills and subjects you would most like to try to improve in Year 9. Discuss with your tutor what you would need to do and the things you would need to change in order to improve in that subject or skill.

Step 2 Together with your tutor agree two or three targets which you both think would be realistic for you to set yourself during Year 9.

Step 3 Draw up an action plan for each of your targets. Think carefully about the various things you need to do in order to achieve a particular target and plan how you are going to achieve it step by step. Give yourself plenty of time to achieve it and set yourself deadlines by which you plan to achieve each step.

State clearly what your aim is, then list the steps you are going to take in order to achieve your goal. Here is the action plan that Gaby drew up in order to try to improve her work in History:

> **Aim:** To get a higher grade in History in Year 9.
>
> **Steps**
> 1. Use more sources when I'm asked to find out about a topic.
> 2. Go to the library and look for information in books, on CD-ROMs and the Internet.
> 3. Make better notes which are focused on the question instead of just copying whole paragraphs from the book.
> 4. Use more evidence to support the points I make in my written work.
> 5. Do my History homework in plenty of time instead of at the last minute.
> 6. Ask Miss Wilks if I can see her once a month to keep a check on how I'm doing.

◖◗ In pairs

Show each other your action plans. Discuss any problems you think you may have in trying to achieve them and what you might do to overcome them.

Index

Answers to quiz on page 92: 1 b, **2** b, **3** b, **4** a, **5** all of them, **6** a, **7** b (the weight of 20 bags of sugar), **8** b (to provide wells and water engineers).